DRIVEWAY
SHOWCASE

ADVANCE PRAISE

"A funny and entertaining photo memoir of our year of the plagues."

—STEPHEN ROSENFIELD, AUTHOR OF *MASTERING STAND-UP: THE COMPLETE GUIDE TO BECOMING A SUCCESSFUL COMEDIAN*, FOUNDER OF THE AMERICAN COMEDY INSTITUTE

"There wasn't much to look forward to during COVID—except for Stephanie Bass's signs. Sharp, clever and spot-on, they made me think, smile, even laugh out loud. You'll look forward to sitting down with this stand-up comic's great book!"

—DAN WOOG, "06880" BLOGGER
www.danwoog06880.com

"Pandemic clouds have silver linings. The plague gave us King Lear *and Calculus. And now COVID gives us* Driveway Showcase. *A poignant and funny lens on the crazy year we survived apart, but somehow together."*

—ETHAN HERSCHENFELD, COMEDIAN/ACTOR. HIS ALBUM "THUG THUG JEW" WENT TO #1 ON iTUNES & AMAZON IN 2020. AVAILABLE ON SPOTIFY, PANDORA & AS A SPECIAL ON YOUTUBE.

"Nothing my mother says about me is true."

—JESSIE JANE SCHWARTZ

"In Star Trek, Captain Kirk kept a log. During COVID-19, Stephanie Bass kept a log, and as so often happened, she expressed what many of us were thinking but were sometimes reluctant to say aloud. Sometimes ADD is a good thing."

—ROBERT SELVERSTONE, PH.D.

"I told this witty and talented woman to 'Go Duck Herself' at the closing of a house I sold her in 2003. Not a typical or auspicious beginning of a friendship, but I just didn't get her humor back then. This charming, witty and insightful perspective of our COVID lives is a must-read for all Liberals. (Righties Beware—Toxic material. You won't get any of it, so what's the point?). This Daily Blackboard approach is perfect for readers and author alike. Stephanie speaks from the heart and hits us with line after line that pierces the heart of the nation's hypocrisy and struggle to deal with a pandemic in the backdrop of abject political turmoil. The laughter and poignant insights resonate throughout."

—MICHAEL LUBELL, WRITER/DAD

"Stephanie Bass has admittedly taken her delightful ADD persona and applied it to her debut book, Driveway Showcase. *As a result, hilarity reigns supreme as Stephanie wows us with her pertinent pictures and prose. This read is guaranteed to keep the pages turning, and our funny bones perpetually tickled and begging for more."*

—JUDITH MARKS-WHITE, *WESTPORT NEWS* HUMORIST/ESSAY COLUMNIST (1985-PRESENT). AUTHOR OF *SEDUCING HARRY & BACHELOR DEGREE* (RANDOM HOUSE/BALLENTINE).

"As COVID upended the lives of my students, I told them, "This may not be the year of college you dreamed of, but you'll be telling stories from this year for the rest of your life." In this delightful book, Stephanie Bass demonstrates this truth. Months in lockdown was not the year she dreamed of, but alone in her home she discovered that humor, insight, and even new friends can be found during the worst of years. And with comedy clubs closed, a front-yard chalkboard sign became her stage. Pull up a chair and "drive by" her yard to see her Driveway Showcase.*"*

—BILL SVELMOE, PROFESSOR OF HISTORY, SAINT MARY'S COLLEGE, NOTRE DAME, INDIANA

DRIVEWAY SHOWCASE

BY

Stephanie Ban

ISBN-13: 978-1-949122-18-3 (Paperback)
ISBN-13: 978-1-949122-19-0 (eBook)

Front cover and back biography photographs by Suzanne Sheridan.
Interior images by Barbara A Lane and Alexandra Koch.
Cover design by Alison McBain and Stephanie Bass.
Interior design by Alison McBain.

Westport, CT
United States of America

First printing July 2021.

To everyone I helped through the 2020 plague
by making you laugh.

You helped me more.

Laughing is what distinguishes us as a higher form of life.

INTRODUCTION

AFTER DECADES OF BEING THE funniest person in the room, at 70 I had found my life's calling as a standup comedian.

My ADD* gift of blurting what everyone was thinking, but were too well-mannered or scared to say out loud, turned out to be the exact talent that made me good at my new craft. Instead of dirty looks and raised eyebrows, I was getting laughs and applause.

I was taking professional workshops at American Comedy Institute in NYC and getting all the open mic stage time I could. I was starting to perfect my stage persona: an exaggerated me, a ditzy divorcee in the ritzy suburbs, smarter than I appeared. I'd moved from 5-minute to 7-minute sets and made it to round #3 of the Funniest Comic in CT. I was getting recognition.

Instead of joining my contemporaries for tai chi at the Senior Center and doing crossword puzzles to keep my brain from crumbling, I had constructed a new life that gave me a rush when I went on stage and admission to a wonderful community.

*Attention Deficit Disorder
(And no, you don't outgrow it.)

INTRODUCTION

When I first showed up—always and obviously the only Westport, CT matron—everyone (way, way younger) was polite enough. But after I "killed" on stage (i.e., got a respectable number of laughs), I was 100% accepted in this generous and supportive group.

Suddenly that was all gone.

March 1st, 2020 was the last time I was in NYC, the last time I saw my 2 best friends and the last time I ate inside a crowded restaurant.

March 8th, 2020 was the last time I got on stage: at Randall's in West Haven, a shit-kicking bar somehow preserved in the 1970s.

March 15th was lockdown.

Everyone's life changed dramatically. You couldn't pace yourself because no one knew how long lockdown would last. Or what our lives would look like when we emerged.

The first 3 months I never left my driveway. I had a once-a-week visit when my kid dropped off groceries. Even that was a stilted do-si-do. In my tiny front yard I danced around on my porch as Jessie left the bags on the stone wall next to the driveway. She danced back to her car as I moved forward to get the food. I sat on the wall, Jessie leaned against her car and we'd have a short visit. Living alone, I was panicked this would be my only human contact.

But that's not what happened.

Early on—isolated, depressed and eager to connect with people—I dug up an old blackboard and started to write jokes.

That's how I invented DRIVEWAY SHOWCASE. No stage, no lights, no audience 2 drinks in who came to laugh. I just started to write jokes on that old blackboard. Every day—or a couple of times a week when the humor wouldn't come easily—I would write my observations and prop my blackboard on a chair in my driveway near the road.

Lots of people had always walked by my cottage on their way to the beach. Now lots of people in cars and on foot stopped to "see" my show. Some took pictures. If they caught me writing in my driveway, they stopped to talk. I started to post on Facebook and Instagram.

That's what saved me in 2020.

Sharing my thoughts and my jokes started as a way to keep my brain working and make non-Zoom or non-text connections with humans. People again told me my humor said what they were feeling; now they added I was helping them get through this difficult time. I realized I was making a positive contribution by bringing humor into their lives. It brought me great joy. Also, presents: beer and wine, lovely notes and sometimes, if I was lucky, toilet paper.

In conversations with these strangers, we always laughed. As time went on it became clear America was in free fall. Our #1 status in the world now referred to the percentage of hospitalizations and deaths. Conversations often got deeper. We voiced our horror at what our politicians were doing or not doing for us, at what was happening to America. Now we wondered when this would be over and what our future world would look like.

Because 2020 was also the year I kept crying. The realization of the meanness that so many people in power showed towards others—people they were supposed to help, people they didn't even know, people they reduced to the color of their skin or the bathroom they wanted to use—made me weep.

Are we going to be different going forward? Kinder? Share the wealth? Agree that science, when backed by truth, is how we're going to fix some of our problems? Become a united America?

I don't know.

INTRODUCTION

What I do know is we need more compassion for everyone wandering the planet and we have to keep laughing.

So welcome to Driveway Showcase, diary of this comedian's year in lockdown.

Enjoy. And don't forget to tip your waitress.

Stephanie Bass
Westport, CT

MARCH-MAY
2020

A FEW WEEKS INTO OFFICIAL lockdown, I was missing my life as a standup comedian. My new adventure was abruptly canceled when the world closed down.

I needed to reinvent my life again, or the only human contact I would have would be seeing my kid and grandkid once a week.

To get me out of my funk and get my brain charged again, I started writing my daily thoughts on an old blackboard. I put it close to the road, sharing it with my "audience" of people walking by.

Here's my 2020 year.

What will we remember about 2020?

By mid-March 2020, President Trump was in year 4 of communicating to the American public mostly via Twitter. Lots of Twitter. Lots and lots of Twitter.

Then the unimaginable happened. A virus spread across the planet. A pandemic. A plague.

Initially we didn't get a lot of information and were only told to stay at home. Everyone in lockdown. Older people were especially scared as, percentage-wise, we had the worst odds.

NY TIMES PERSON: PLEASE LEAVE SOME GOOD NEWS.

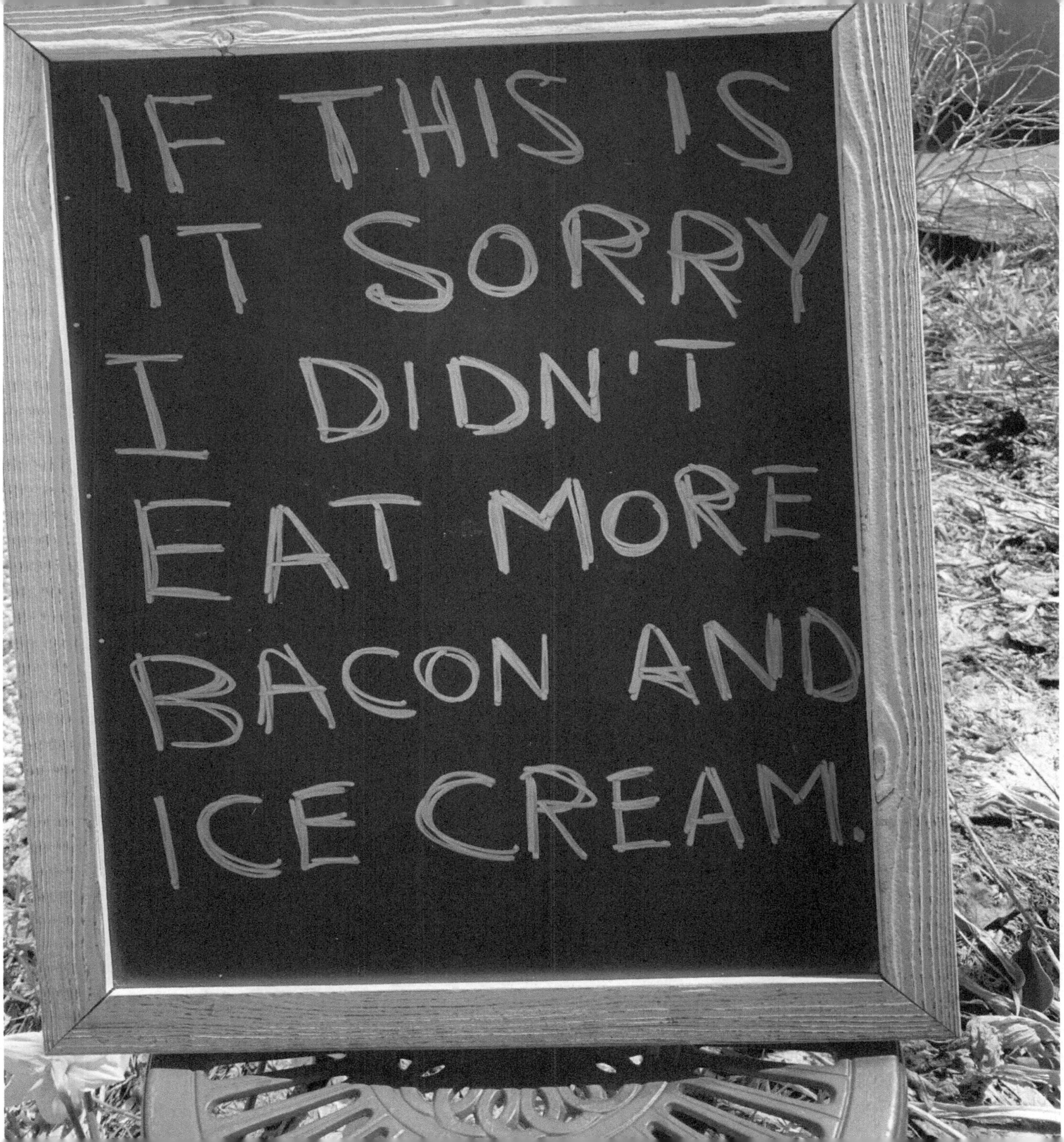
IF THIS IS
IT SORRY
I DIDN'T
EAT MORE
BACON AND
ICE CREAM.

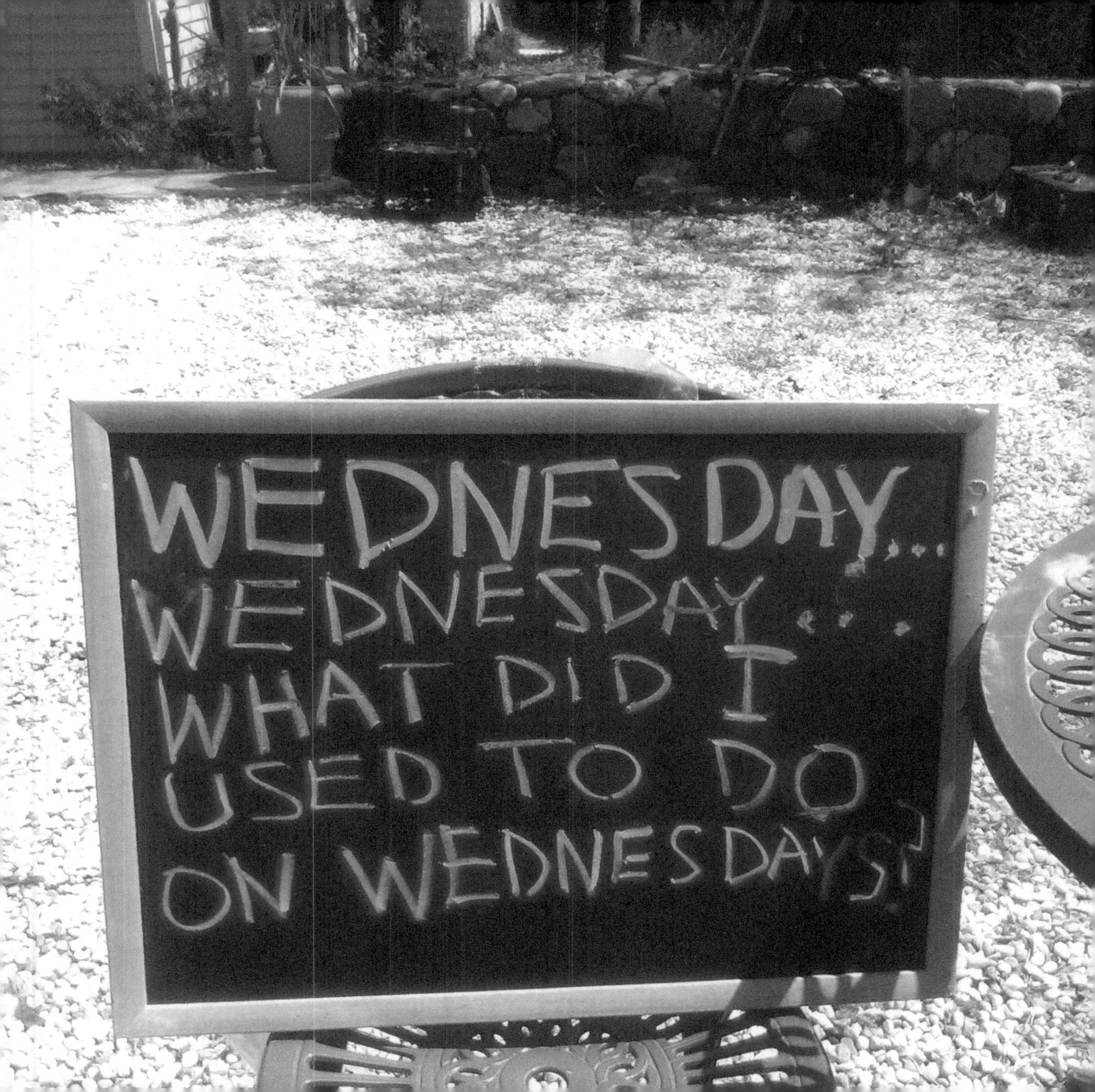
WEDNESDAY...
WEDNESDAY...
WHAT DID I
USED TO DO
ON WEDNESDAYS?

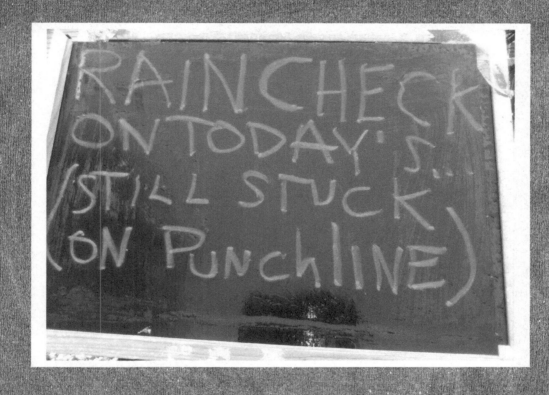

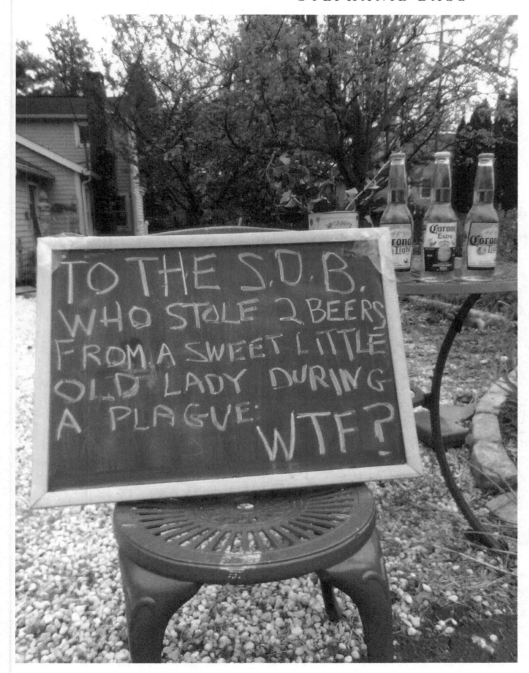

To simulate the feel of the comedy clubs I was missing, I had left 5 beers on the table next to my blackboard. When one member of my "audience" took the "two-drink minimum for admittance" too literally, I had to call him on it.

PRACTICING FLIRTING WITH THE MAILMAN, PROPANE GUY AND RANDOM MEN WALKING BY IN CASE I EVER GET OUT OF HERE

As time went on, I started to buy into the concept that the passersby were my audience. Some of my "regulars" said they stopped every day just to get their laugh fix and were disappointed when I didn't have a new bit by 10 a.m., which I had set as my showtime to give structure to my days in solitary confinement. On this day, I couldn't think of a punchline and wanted to let them know I was still working on material and had not forgotten them.

HAPPY
MOTHER'S
DAY!!!
(RE-INSTATED KID
WHO FORGOT
BACON BACK IN
WILL.)

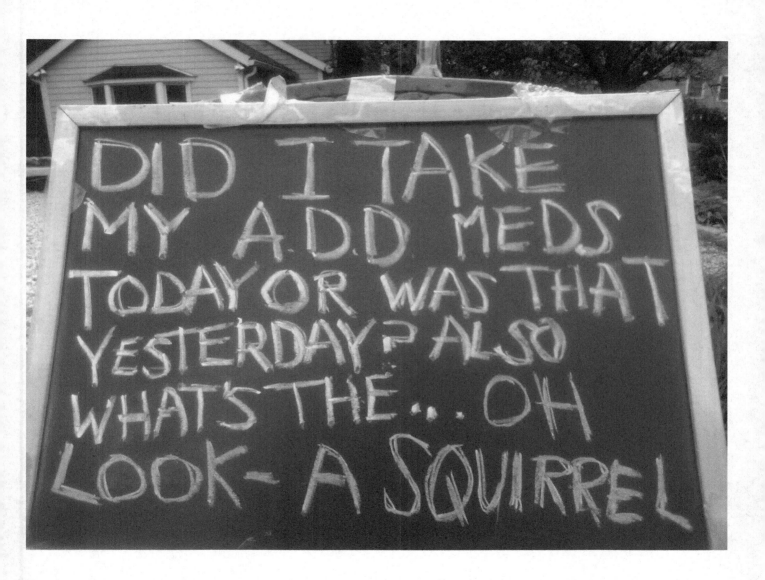

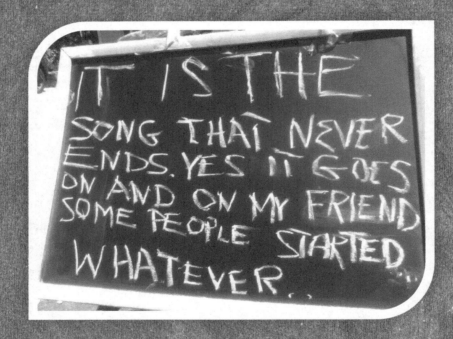

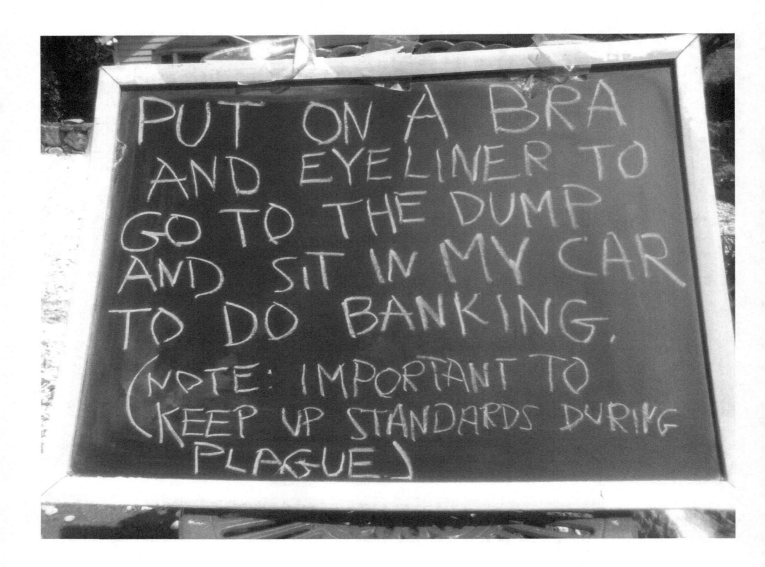

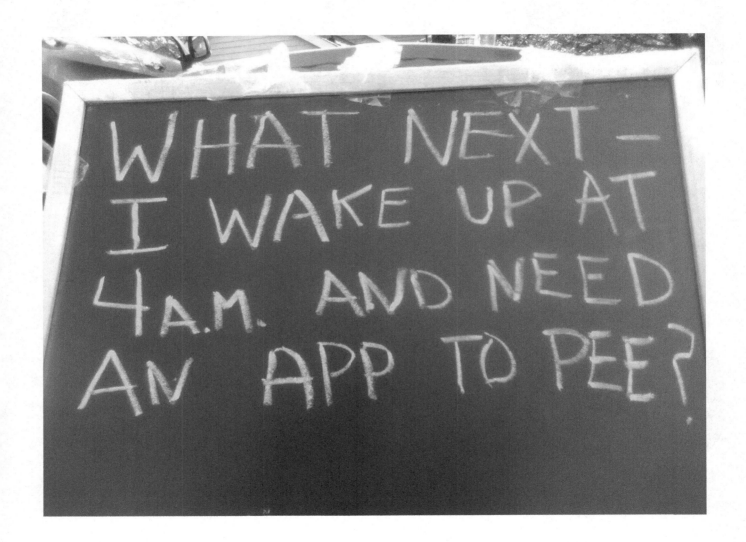

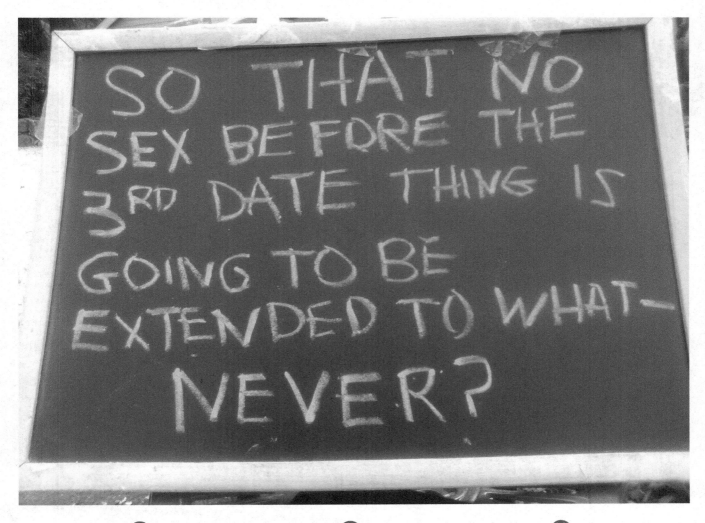

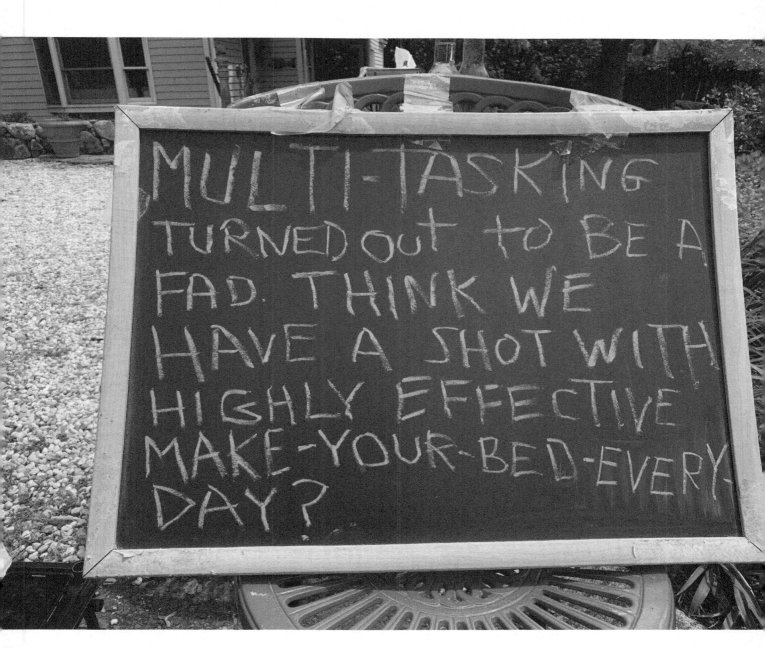

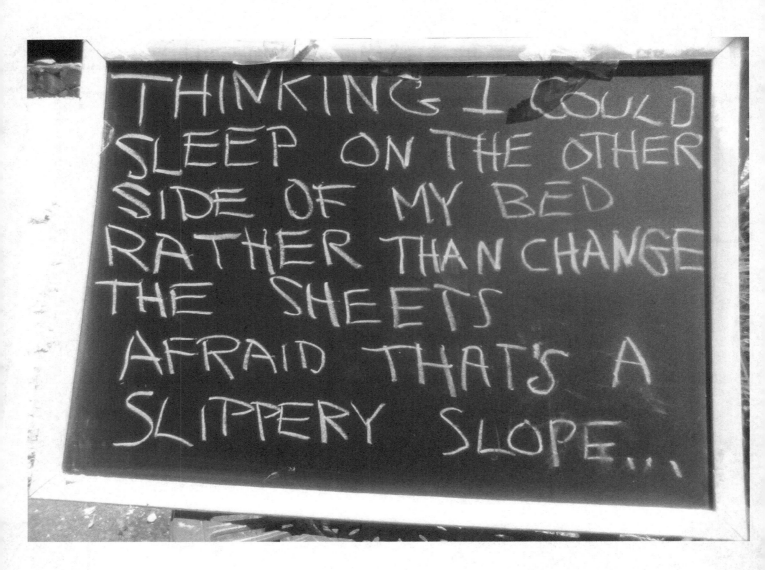

NEW WORLD:
  REMEMBER TO PEE
BEFORE LEAVING HOUSE FOR
FOR MORE THAN 3 ERRANDS
AS USING PUBLIC
BATHROOMDOMS
SOUNDS LIKE A
27 STEP PROJECT.

NEW WORLD:
AS THEY OPEN
UP MORE STUFF,
ON EXACTLY WHAT
DAY DO I HAVE
TO KNOW EXACTLY
WHAT DAY IT IS
EVERY DAY?

My grandson Robert, who showed up with the personality of a frat boy 5 beers in, kept me sane during lockdown.

JUNE-AUGUST
2020

Two Crises and Surging Anger Convulse U.S.: A Pandemic and Police Violence

~NY Times, June 1, 2020

U.S. at a precipice as demonstrations intensify

~Washington Post, June 1, 2020

As the world got darker and uglier, as we watched the 9-minute tape of George Floyd killed on May 25th over and over, a lot of us thought: *This is enough; this time we have to make a change.*

This started with a conversation in my head. I've always thought that we don't learn our moral codes by what we hear once a week in a church or a synagogue or a mosque. We learn by what we hear our parents say every night around the kitchen table. If they denigrate people of color or people who immigrated a generation after they did or trash talk any differences, this is what their children learn.

Fox News must have especially disgusted me that day.

Westport always had a reputation of being very artsy: populated by musicians, theatre people, movie stars, painters, art directors and writers. Very liberal politically, sexually and accepting of all types of people. By the time I arrived in 1991, a tremendous wave of new Wall Street $$$ and monster McMansions had become pervasive and it was hard to see what was left of the good ol' days. After George Floyd was murdered, Westport seemed to be galvanized into action; in marches and gatherings and speeches. In my town I saw a spirit of *enough; we won't be silent at injustice.*

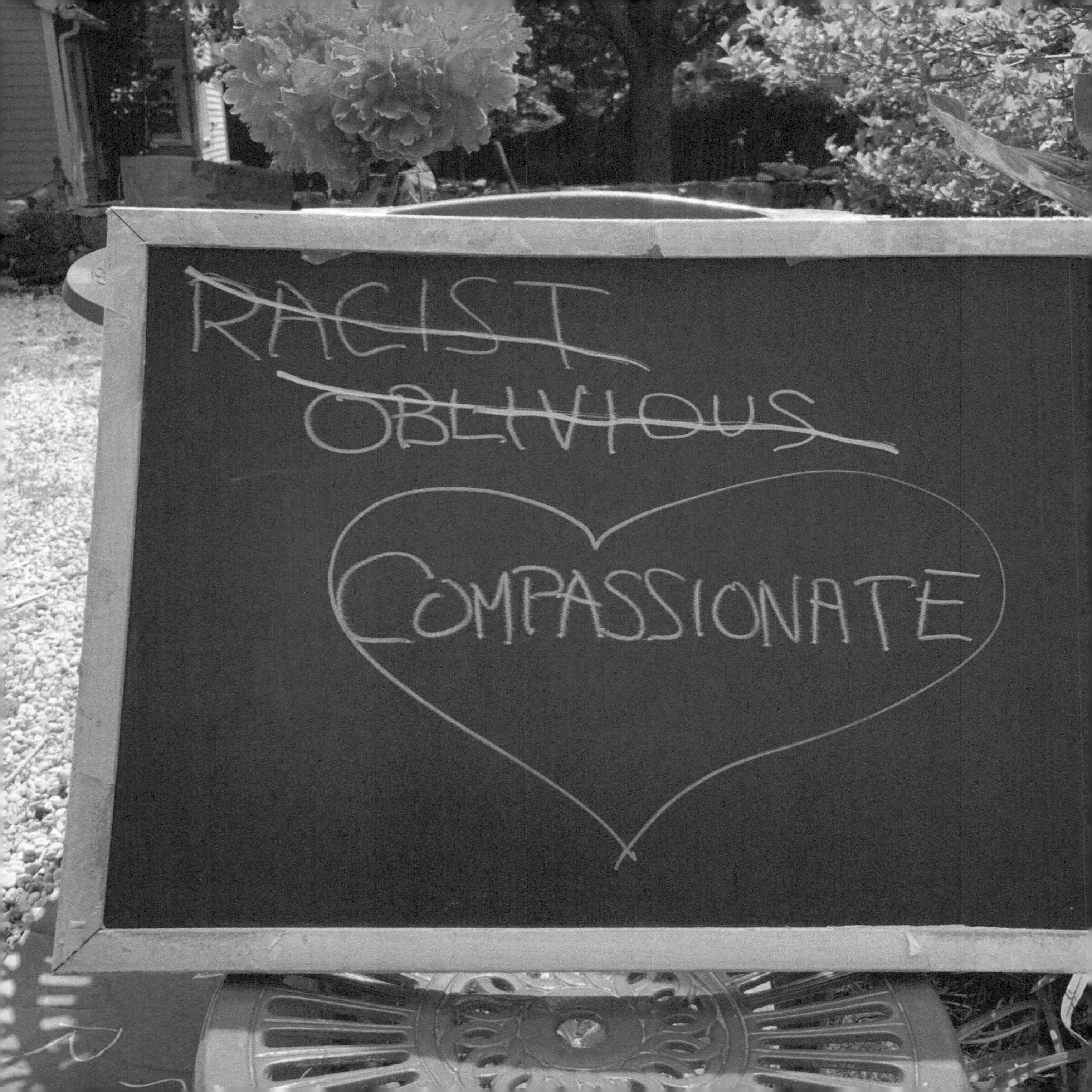
RACIST
OBLIVIOUS
COMPASSIONATE

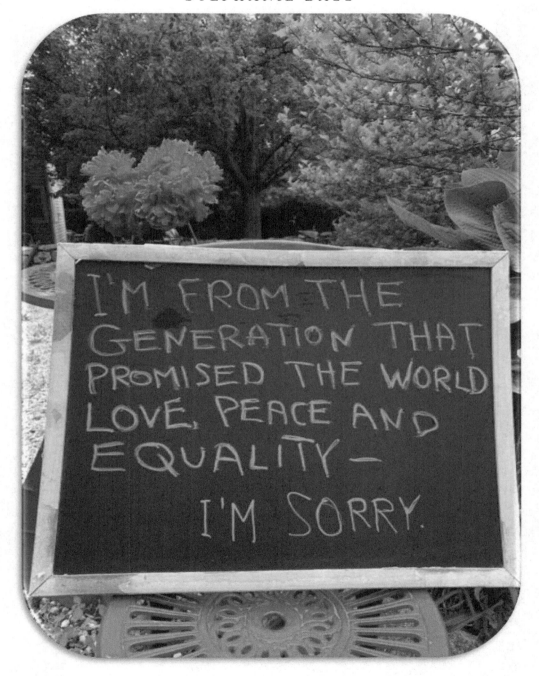

1ST TIME IN 3 MONTHS:
WENT FACE-TO-FACE
MEETING WITH
PEOPLE NOT RELATED
TO ME. THRILLING
EVEN AT 6 FEET !!!
(HAD TO RUSH HOME
AS HAVEN'T
MASTERED 23
STEPS TO USE
PUBLIC
RESTROOMS.)

LIFE HACK:

STRETCH 1 TANK
OF GAS 3 MONTHS—
HAVE A MANIACAL
PUTZ IN CHARGE
OF MANAGING A
F©?!☆KING PLAGUE.

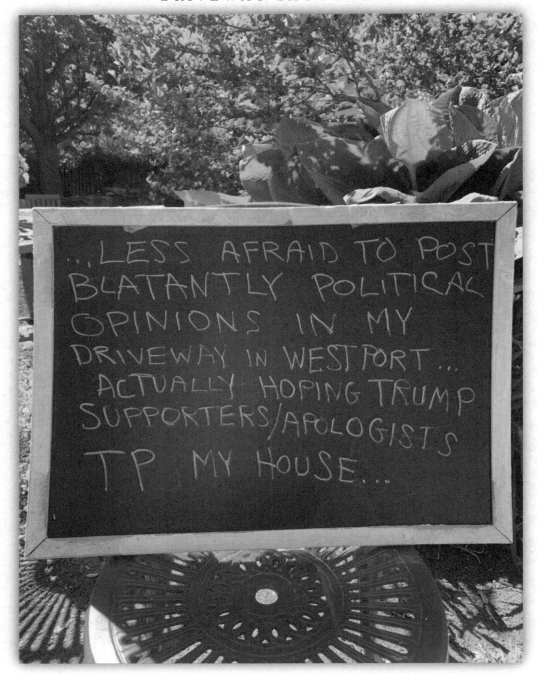

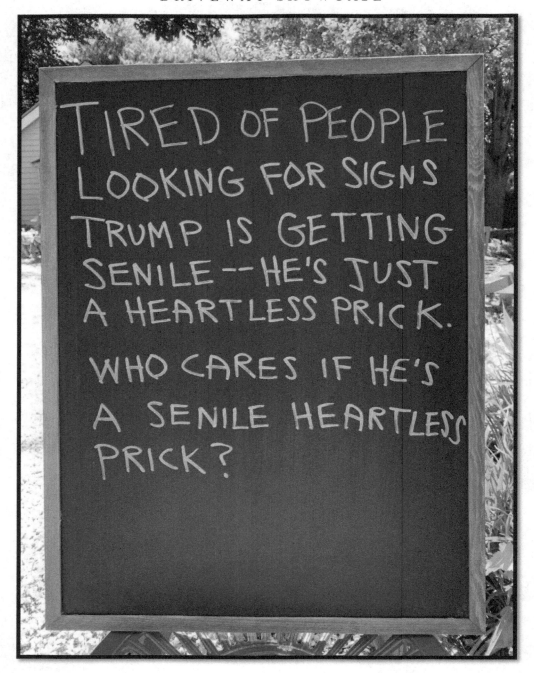

MY GENERATION SAID NEVER TRUST ANYONE OVER 30. MAYBE WE WERE RIGHT.

HAPPY
FATHER'S
DAY
(TURN OFF THE NEWS
AND ENJOY THE DAY)

By now, my filters were pretty much shot. Also, strangely, while dropping "F" bombs was still not okay in many places in society, somehow—and I have no idea who makes up these rules—WTF was not only acceptable, it was considered kinda "cute." My response here was to President Trump responding to criticism of his handling the pandemic, measured by the percentage of Americans testing positive for COVID-19. We were in the lead of other countries, *but not in a good way*. And remember, the leader of the free world NEVER told us to wear masks, somehow turning it into a political issue. This is the only time I quote him; once was enough.

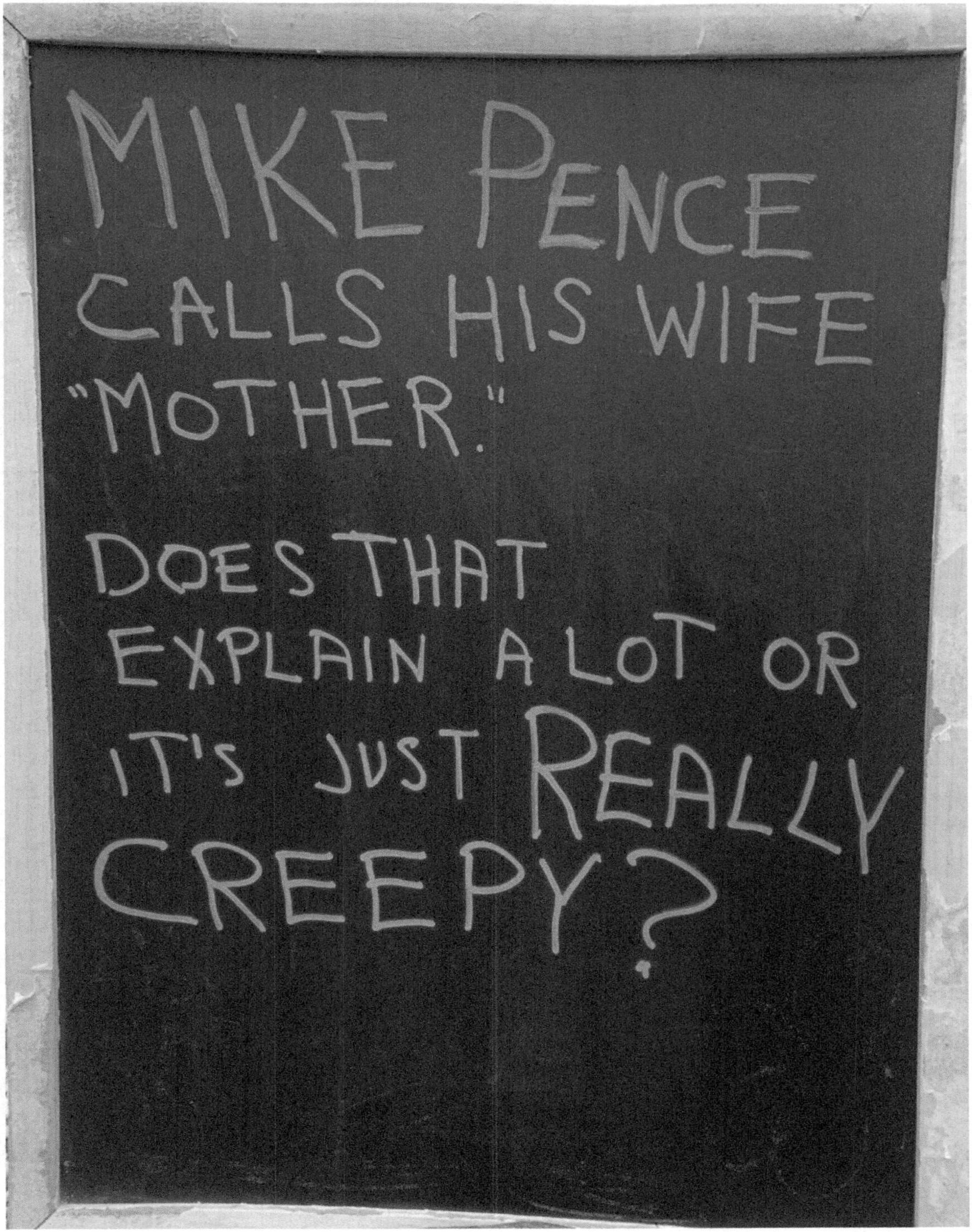
MIKE PENCE
CALLS HIS WIFE
"MOTHER."
DOES THAT
EXPLAIN A LOT OR
IT'S JUST REALLY
CREEPY?

THANK YOU AMAZON AND SEPHORA FOR BRINGING JOY AND MASCARA INTO MY LIFE.

FOR A COUNTRY TOO
DUMB TO MATCH THE #
OF HOT DOGS TO THE #
OF ROLLS IN A PACKAGE
HOW WE GONNA FIX:

☐ RACISM

☐ PLAGUE

☐ POLITICAL
CORRUPTION

☐ $$$ INEQUALITY

☐ GLOBAL
WARMING

☐ ... ☐ ... ☐ ... ☐ ...

These 33 Countries Have Banned U.S. Travelers

~*Forbes*, July 2020

As the world watches America in free fall, we are banned from traveling anywhere.

WATCHED 2 HOURS OF NEWS THIS MORNING — BIG MISTAKE. TAKING THE DAY OFF FROM FINDING CLEVER WAYS OF SAYING TRUMP IS GARBAGE

WHEN MY KID
WAS LITTLE. ON
THE 1ST DAY OF
SCHOOL EVERY YEAR
SHE SAID, "182 DAYS
OF SCHOOL LEFT. (A
MATH GENIUS.) COULD
SOMEONE FIGURE
OUT # OF DAYS 'TIL
ELECTION AND # OF DAYS
'TIL TG!!?✦P OUT? (I'M
TOO DEPRESSED AND WAS
MARKETING MAJOR.)

...MUST HAVE PRESSED THE WRONG BUTTON—DISCONNECTED SIRI — NOW I'M GONNA BE AS DUMB AS ½ OF TEXAS

I never used this one. I was working on crystallizing the concept when my kid said it looked like a penis. I tried adding that reference but it still didn't work. [Note: misspelling.] Also I don't work blue (show biz jargon for "dirty").

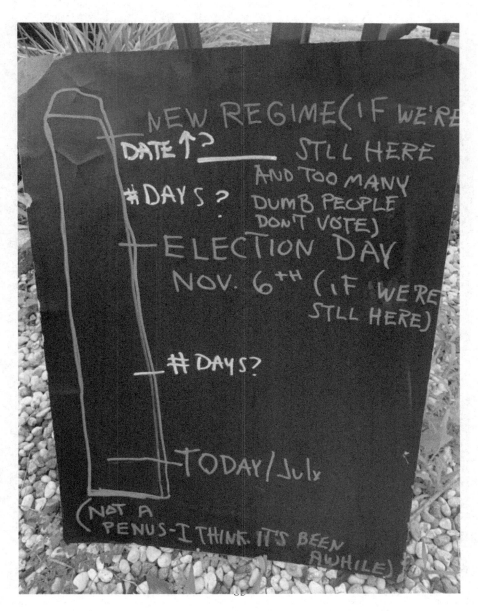

...GIVE CREDIT WHERE
CREDIT IS DUE... TRUMP
CORRECT:
AMERICA #1 !!!

PANDEMIC:
WORLDWIDE: 13 million
AMERICA: 3.3 million

WEAR A
MASK?

LET'S ALL
MAKE A VOW
NOT TO BUY ANY
BOOKS BY
REPUBLICAN
POLITICIANS WHO
ARE GONNA FIND
G-D SOON AFTER
NOVEMBER ELECTIONS

Not *everyone* loved my material. I got some "hecklers"—always 2 or 3 old white men (women just averted their eyes). I would smile when they said, "But the market is up!"—not engaging in conversation, knowing a list of the dreadful things Trump was doing would not change their opinions.

Once I found my black-board, table and chair thrown into the rho-dodendrons lining my driveway. This was my response.

USED TO SAY
EVEN BAD
PIZZA IS GOOD.

THEN SOME
YOYO INVENTED
CAULIFLOWER
PIZZA DOUGH.
IT SUCKS.
SERIOUSLY

JULY 16:
"SCIENCE SHOULD NOT
STAND IN THE WAY
OF ALLOWING SCHOOLS
TO REOPEN."
        -KAYLEIGH McNANY
        WH PRESS SECRETARY

JULY 19:

"WTF??!!?

        -STEPHANIE BASS
        CITIZEN TRYING
        TO HOLD ON TO
        SANITY

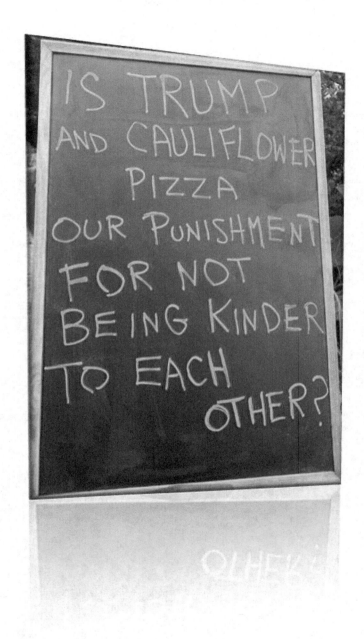

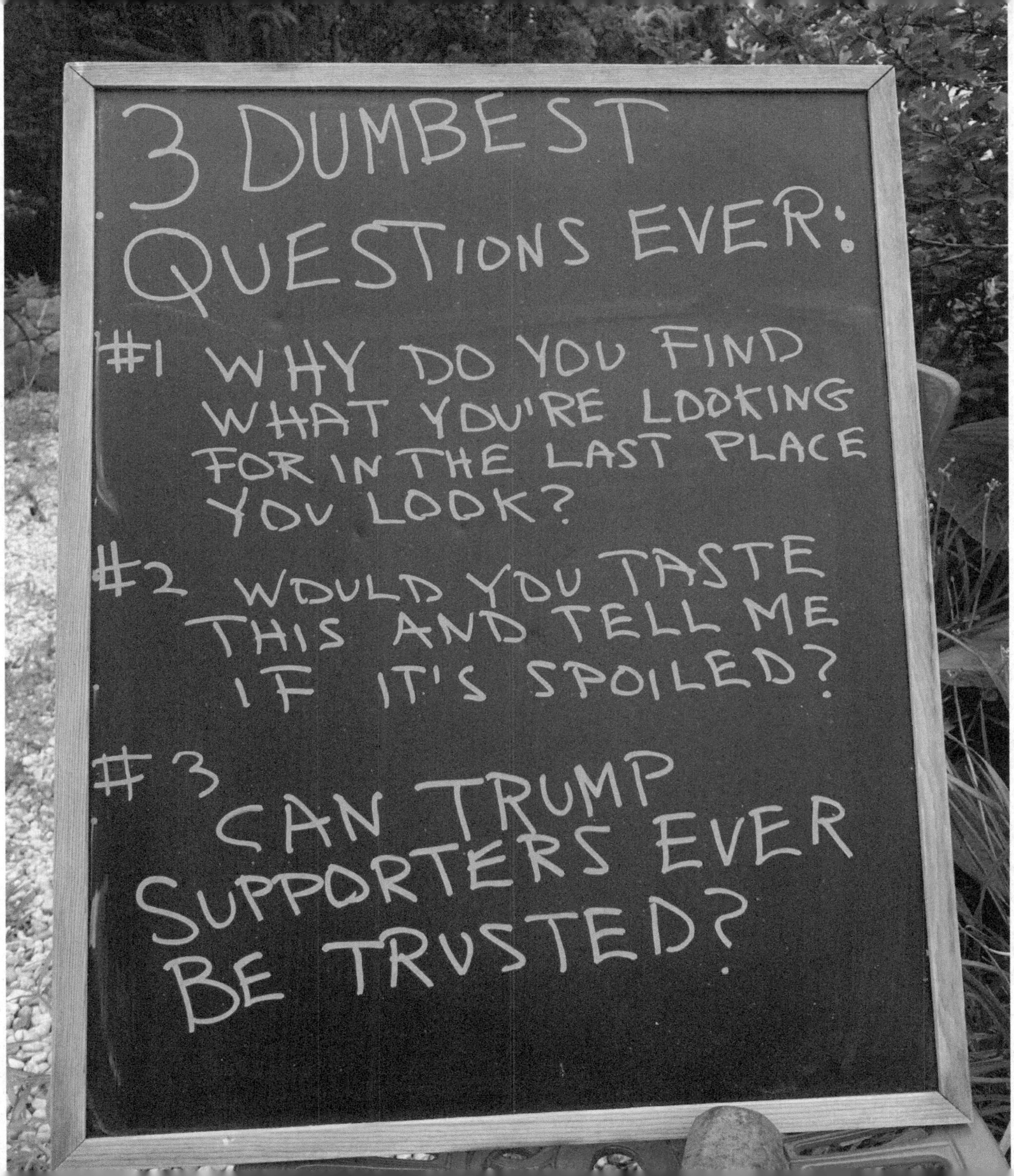
3 DUMBEST
QUESTIONS EVER:
#1 WHY DO YOU FIND
WHAT YOU'RE LOOKING
FOR IN THE LAST PLACE
YOU LOOK?
#2 WOULD YOU TASTE
THIS AND TELL ME
IF IT'S SPOILED?
#3
CAN TRUMP
SUPPORTERS EVER
BE TRUSTED?

INSTEAD OF
WRITING HIS
NAME, LET'S
REFER TO HIM
AS T©&!!!P -
LIKE WE WRITE
F©&!!!K SO WE
DON'T SULLY
THE CHILDREN.

JULY 29th
TO DO LIST:

1. MAKE BED

2. FORGIVE MYSELF FOR NOT DOING ANYTHING ON MY MARCH 29th TO DO LIST

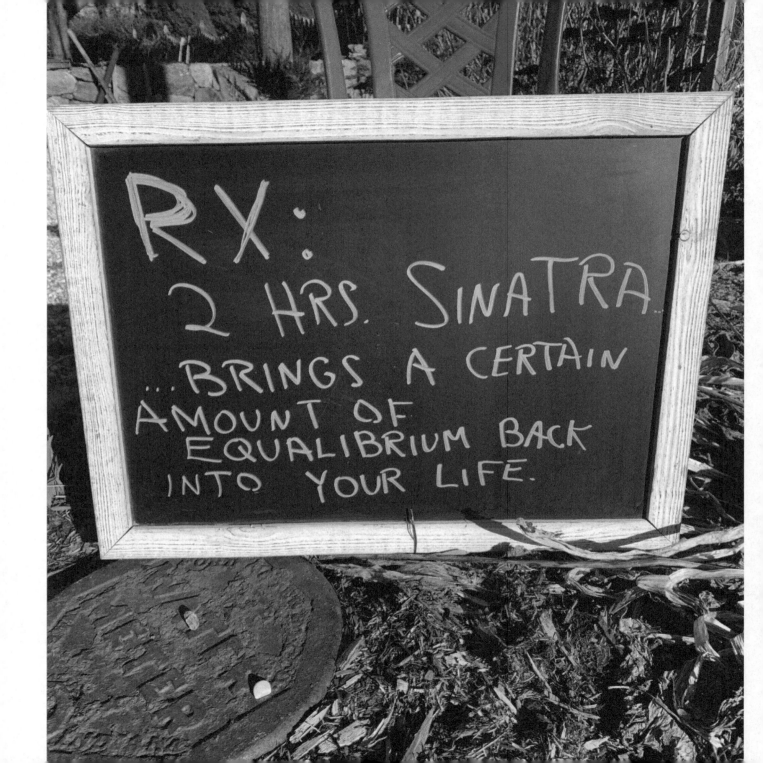

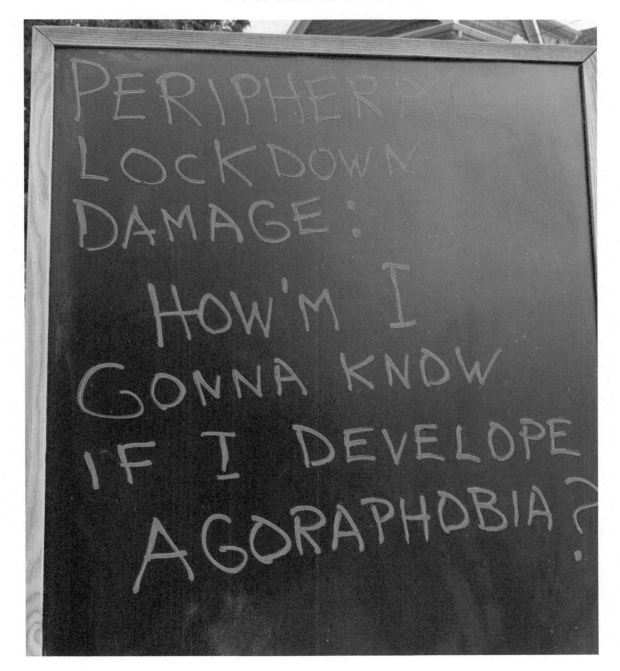

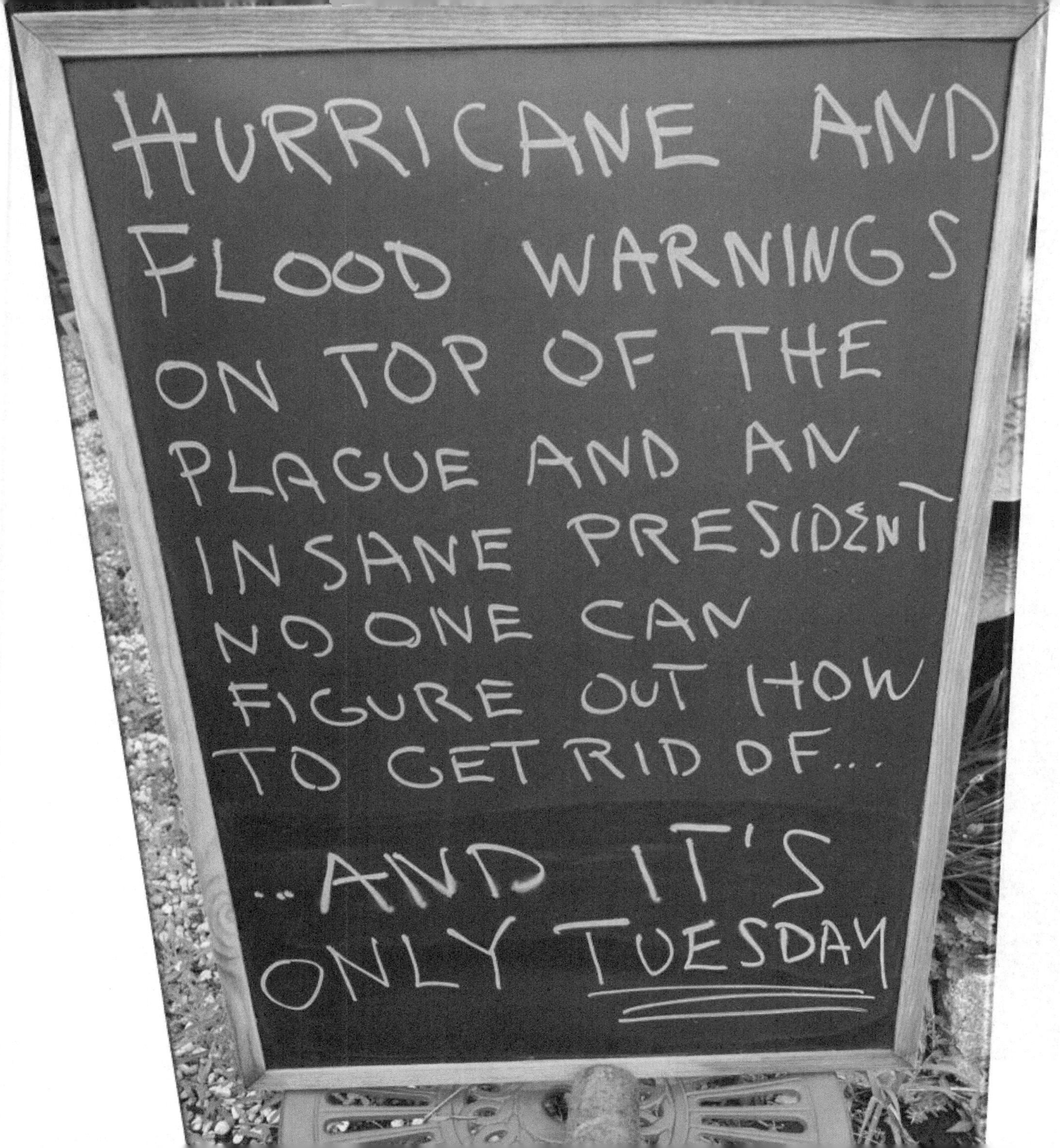

HURRICANE AND
FLOOD WARNINGS
ON TOP OF THE
PLAGUE AND AN
INSANE PRESIDENT
NO ONE CAN
FIGURE OUT HOW
TO GET RID OF...

...AND IT'S
ONLY TUESDAY

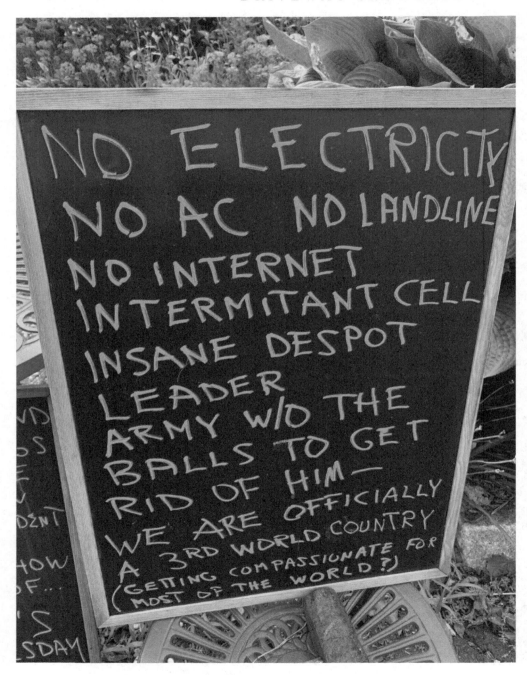

After a severe storm, the CEO of Eversource (income: $19 million/year), the monopoly doling out electricity in the Northeast, does a terrible job—no response to thousands without power, days move into one week, then 2… So we have a jerk in charge of our country, a worldwide plague and now our Häagan-Dazs is melting…?

BACK FROM 2
NIGHTS AT HOTEL-
CHAIN SAWS PUSHED
ME OVER THE
EDGE.

SETTING: HOTEL DINING
ROOM
WAITER: ANYTHING
ELSE I CAN?
DO FOR YOU?
ME: GET NIXON OUT
OF WH.*
...MAYBE I SHOULD
HAVE STAYED LONGER...
(TRUE CONVERSATION)

Wonderful documentary, *Grey Gardens* (1975) by the Maysle Brothers. About Jackie Kennedy's crazy high-society dropout cousins, a mother and daughter who lived in squalor, with lots of cats, in the Hamptons. Eventually, it was made into a Broadway musical (2006) and a movie (2009).

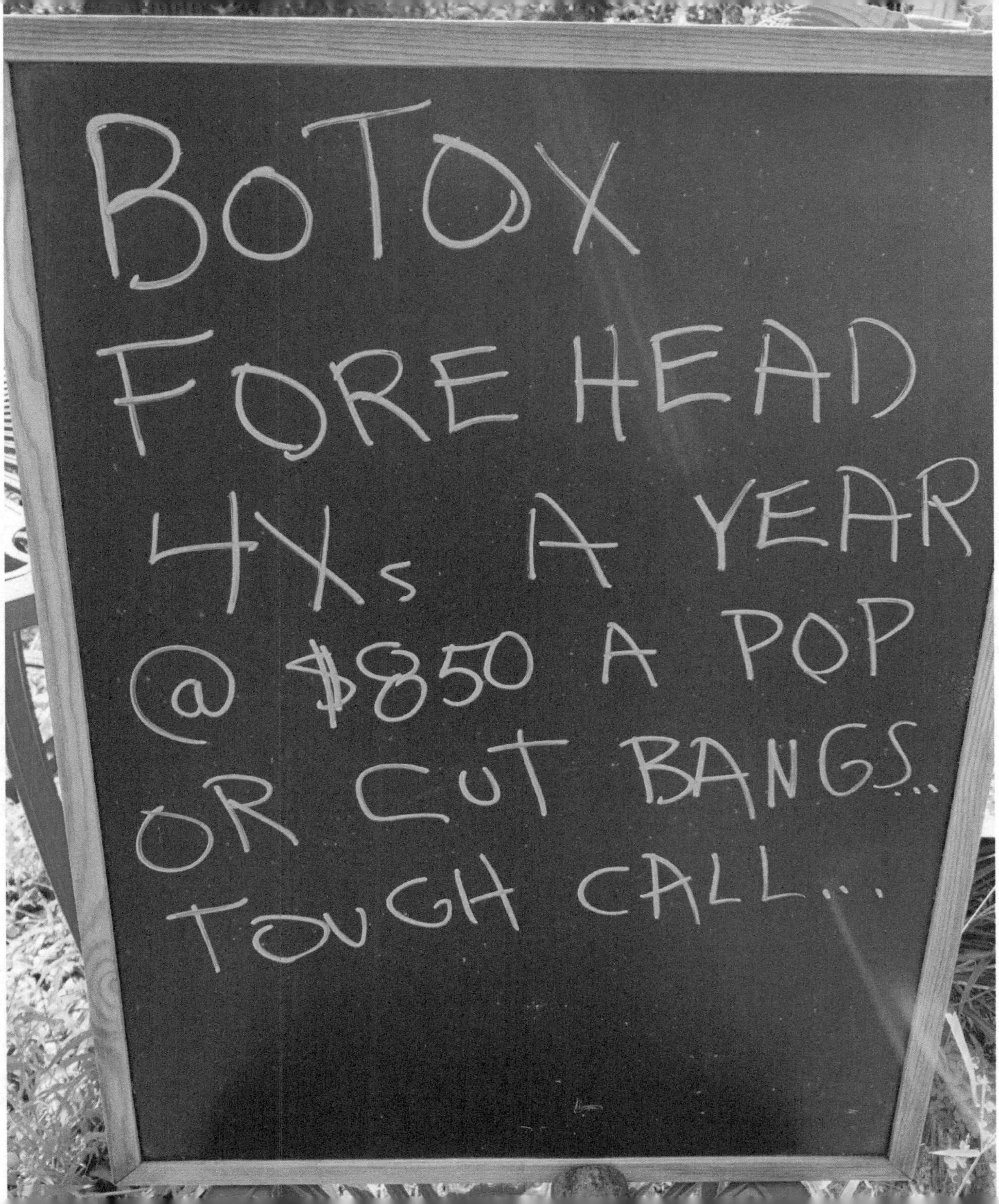
BoTOX
FOREHEAD
4Xs A YEAR
@ $850 A POP
OR CUT BANGS...
TOUGH CALL...

To graduate from high school, I had to take at least one science course. Hating any course I could not BS an essay to pass, I found the one with the not-going-on-to-higher-education-guys. As the class covered the various names for trees, different-sized water formations and rocks, it acquired the name I used on my board.

As I got progressively disheartened by the behavior of Republicans, I fantasized that my old classmates must have entered politics…

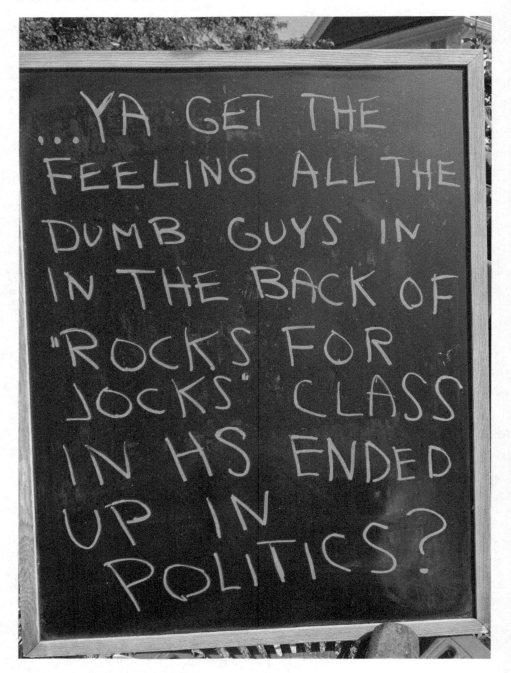

CLEVER COMPLAINING
CANCELLED DUE
TO RAIN.

BACK TOMORROW

(STILL LOTS OF
STUFF I'M
PISSED AT.)

I REMEMBER MY MOTHER SAYING SHE REALIZED SHE WAS OLD WHEN ALL THE DOCTORS AND FIREMEN LOOKED SO YOUNG.

WHAT WAS SHE DOING HANGING OUT WITH FIREMEN?

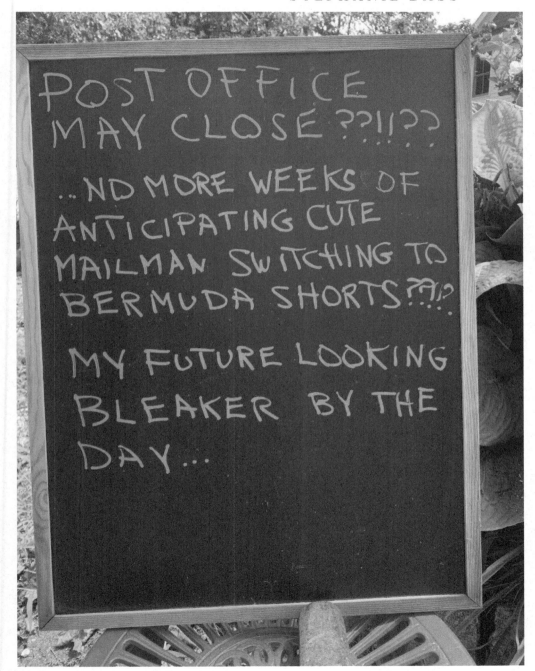

Trump admits he is under-mining USPS to make it harder to vote by mail

~*The Guardian*, August 2020

Trump dismantling the P.O. threatens to destroy my brief flirtations—masked and socially distanced—I enjoy with my hunky mailman.

6 months in and contemplating the existential question of our time: are men, children of political cronies, blonde bimbo apologists for Trump lying or do they believe this crap? Without access to information, the administration spokes-people seemed to both make stuff up and be increasingly hostile to members of the press.

As the system of press conferences disintegrated before our eyes, the only info we got was from more and more dis-orienting Tweets and from Fox News. They both reported "the news" and fed it to Trump.

(Note: by now my spelling had begun to disintegrate...)

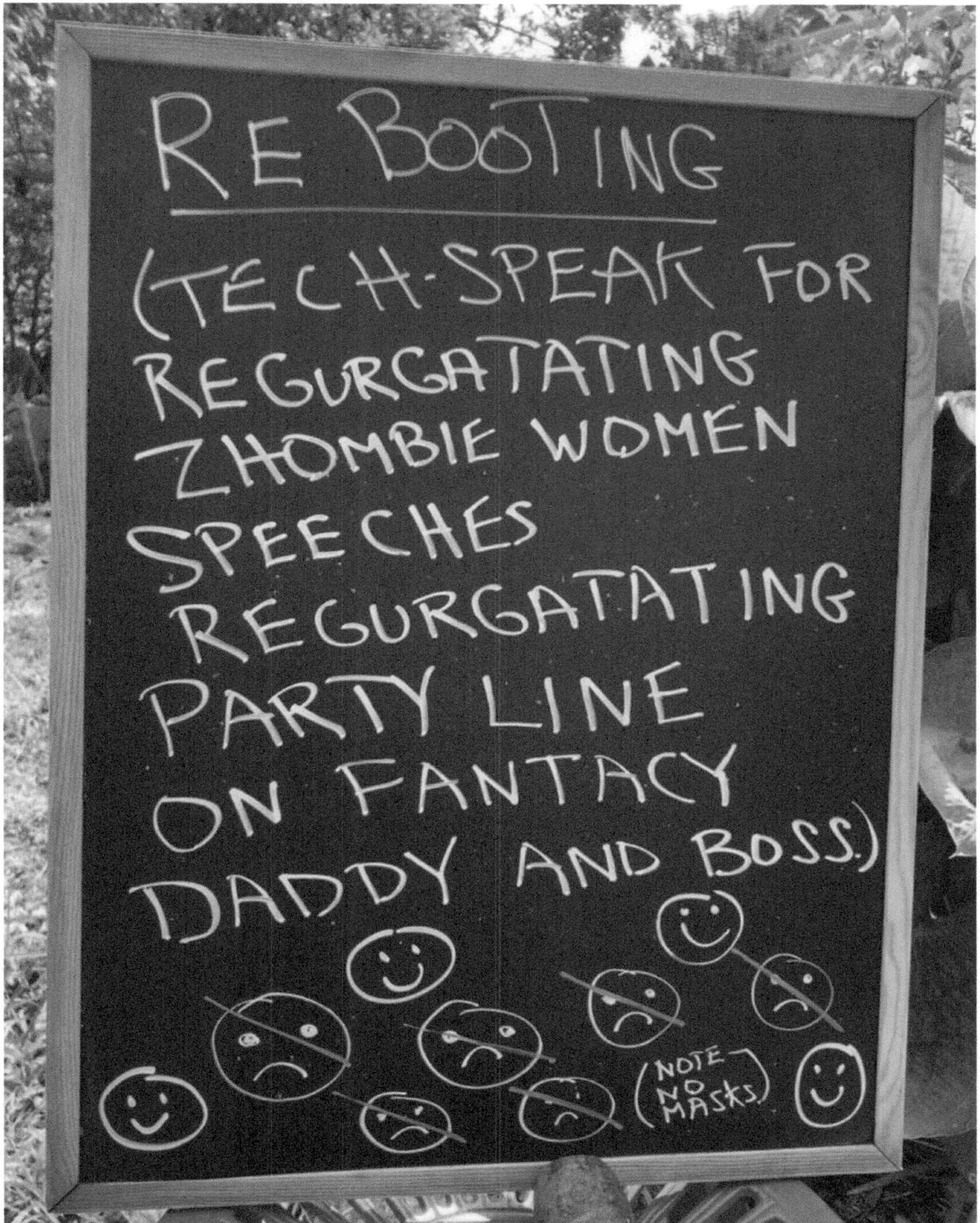
RE BOOTING
(TECH-SPEAK FOR
REGURGATATING
ZHOMBIE WOMEN
SPEECHES
REGURGATATING
PARTY LINE
ON FANTACY
DADDY AND BOSS.)
(NOTE NO MASKS.)

SEPTEMBER-NOVEMBER
2020

APRRARENTLY IT IS OFFICIALLY AUTUMN. EVERY OTHER ITEM AT TRADER JOE'S IS PUMPKIN SOMETHING PERSONALLY I THINK PUMPKIN TAMPONS A LITTLE OVER THE TOP, BUT I'M NOT THEIR TARGOT AUDIENCE.

DEPRESSED.
TEXTED MY KID:
 SAID TO WALK ½ HOUR
 EVERY MORNING.
FACETIMED MY
SHRINK:
 SAID TO WALK ½ HOUR
 EVERY MORNING.
 (CHARGED ME
 $250.)
 ONLY
 (KID CHARGED
 ME $50.)

IRS SENT ME A
BILL FOR $38.72+
INTEREST FOR
UNDERPAYING 2018
TAXES AND THEY
CAN'T NAIL TRUMP
AND FAMILY FOR
YEARS OF CHEATING
ON PERSONAL AND
BUSINESS TAXES IN
THE $$$MILLIONS
??????????

GOOD NEWS:
   MOVED UPSTAIRS
TO GUEST ROOM
TO COMBAT
CABIN FEVER

_____

BAD NEWS:
   ME, MY IPHONE
AND MY CHARGER
ARE NEVER ON
THE SAME FLOOR.

STEPHANIE BASS

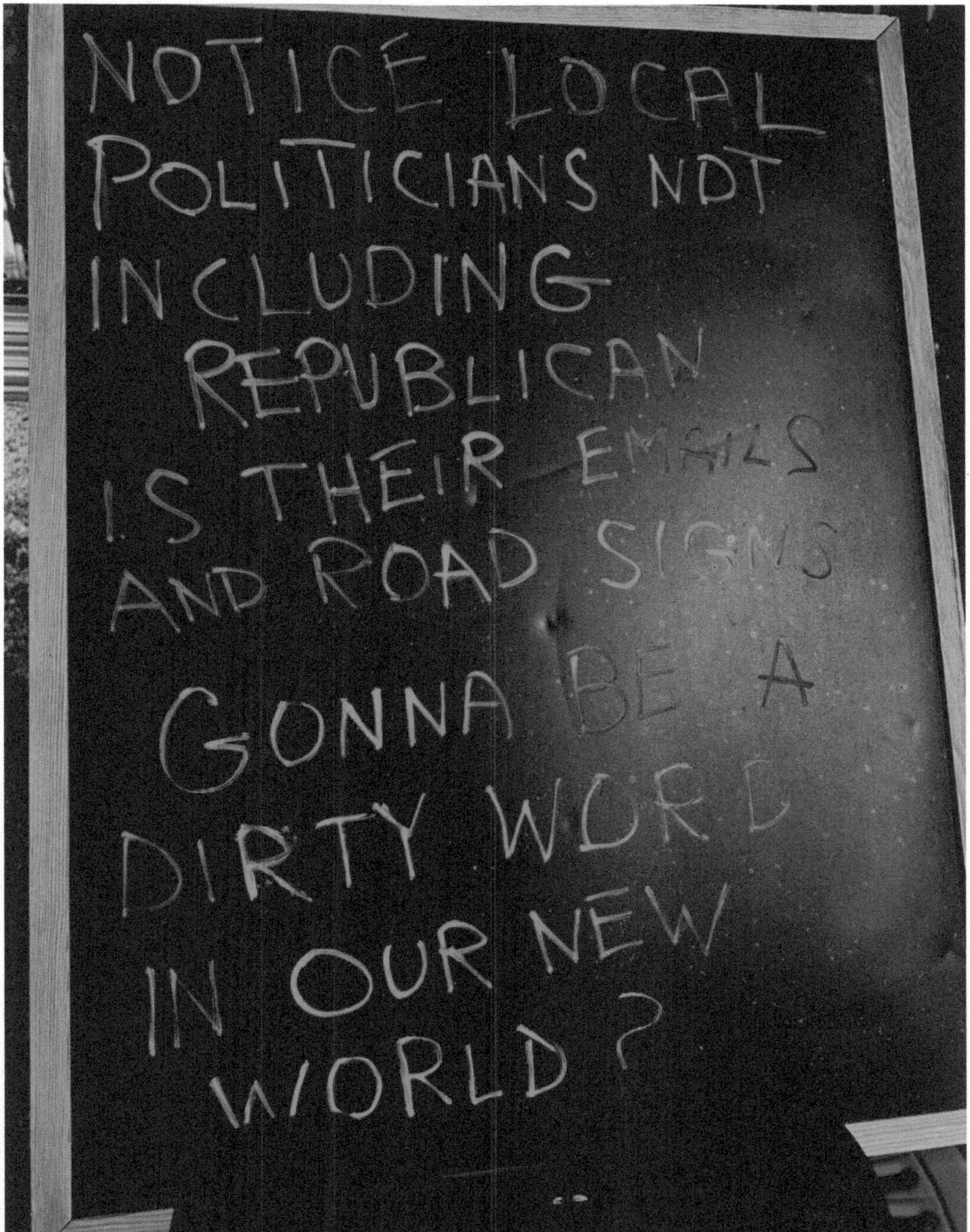

TO REPUBLICAN
POLITICIANS NOT
SLITHERING
AWAY FROM TRUMP
YA STILL
GOT A LINE
IN THE SAND?
ONE AND ALL:
(WEAR A MASK)

LOVE MY 2YEAR
OLD GRANDSON
TO THE BONE SO
OK PIZZA SAUCE
NOT COMING
OFF MY COUCH
BUT WHEN HE
WRECKS MY
1,000 PIECE
PUZZLE 700+ PIECES
CONNECTED I HAVE TO
CUT HIM OUT OF MY
WILL.

Months of isolation; going feral. 180+ meals all alone have shot my table manners; I was worried my language skills were deteriorating too, making me unfit for human company.

"Sanforized" was a popular marketing term started in the 70s by dry cleaners, a bastardized word that came from "sanitary." Sometimes I feel we over-clean, thereby taking the personality out of things.

TRUMP IS A
POOPHEAD.

LISTENING TO
HIS RANTS
FOR 4 YEARS
HAS TURNED ME
INTO A CRANKY
6 YEAR OLD.

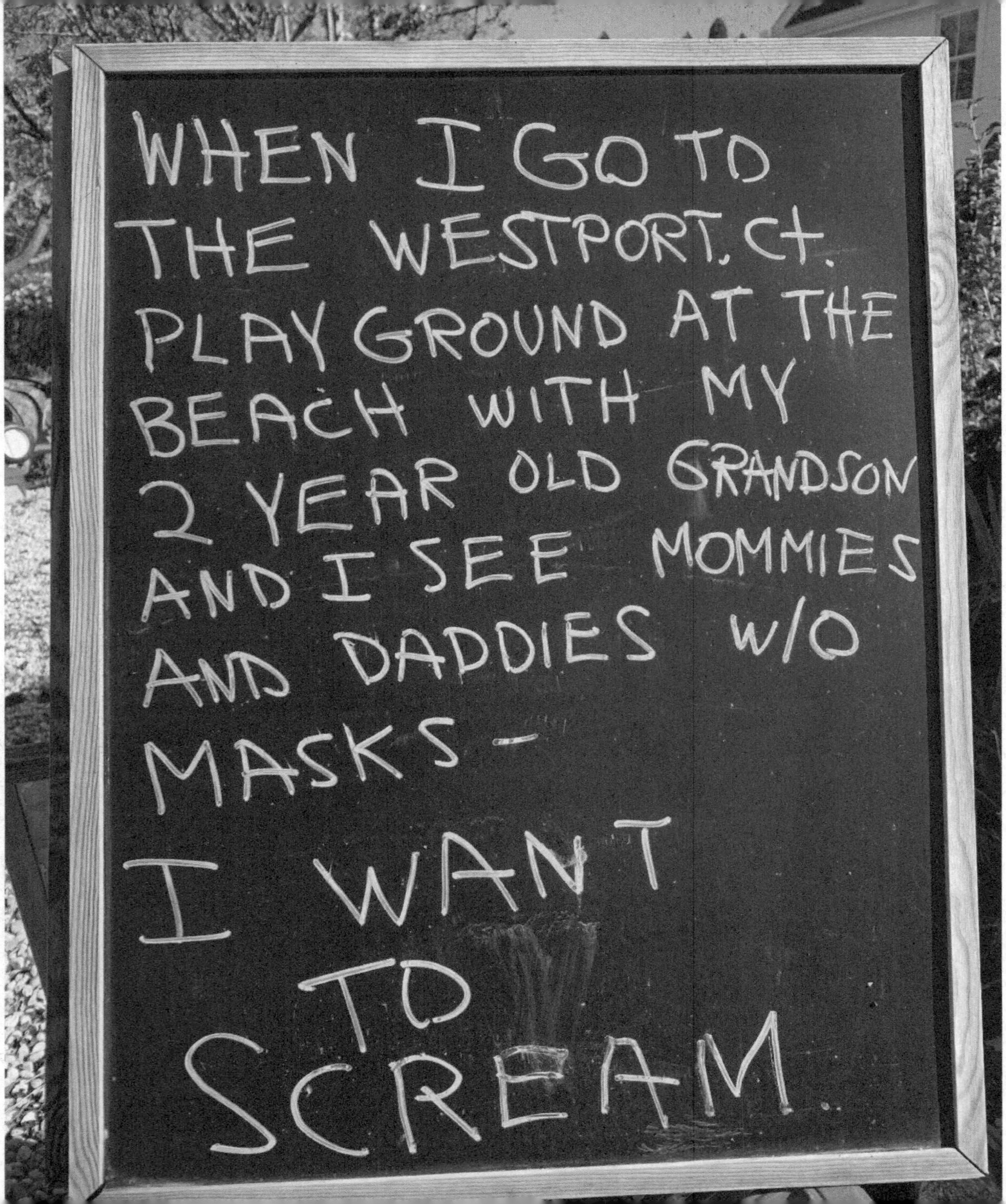
WHEN I GO TO
THE WESTPORT, Ct.
PLAYGROUND AT THE
BEACH WITH MY
2 YEAR OLD GRANDSON
AND I SEE MOMMIES
AND DADDIES W/O
MASKS -
I WANT
TO
SCREAM.

REMEMBER
THE GOOD OLD
DAYS WHEN
YOU LOOKED
FORWARD TO
READING THE
SUNDAY NYTs?
STONE
GOOD
NEWS

EVER FEEL
LIKE YOU'RE
IN A BAD MOVIE
AND YA CAN'T
FIND THE DAMN
CLICKER???

I wanted to support the good guys until I was getting 20+ requests a week for $$$. It was overwhelming the number of requests we all got in this tragic year. I always make jokes but I write checks to organizations who provided food for those in need.

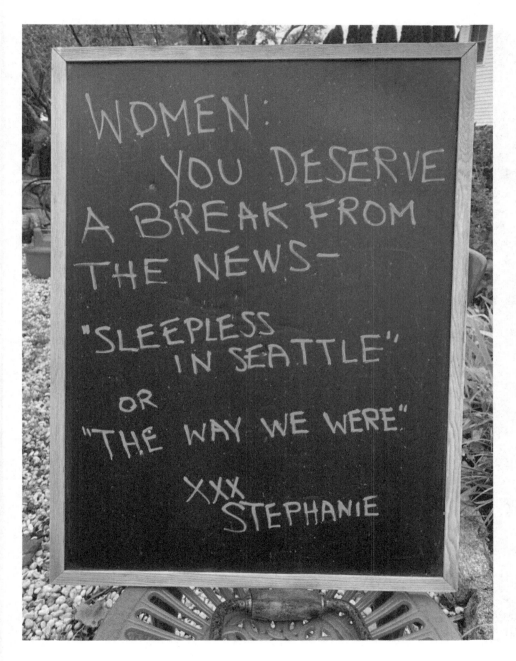

3 days straight of the MSNBC Holy Trinity—Rachel Maddow + Lawrence O'Donnell + Brian Williams—and my brain is cooked with the horrors in the news. My kid—and my shrink—said to stop watching so much news. I passed on the message to my audience…

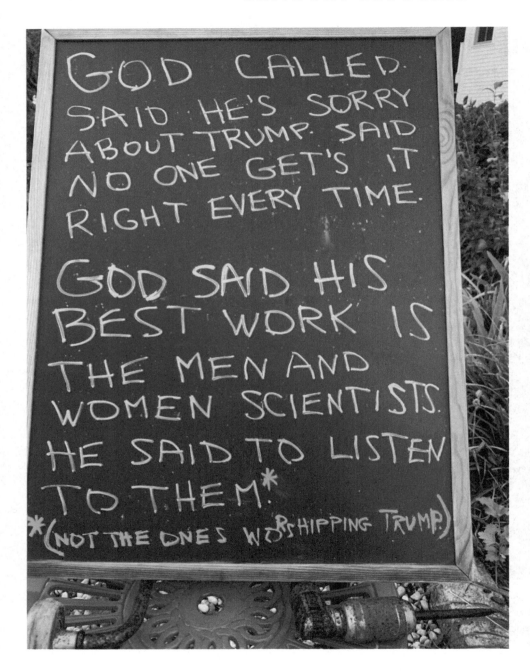

With Republicans frequently holding up a shield of God to defend their lack of compassion towards their constituents, I thought a different take on His message might be a good idea.

CHILDREN (AND
PARENTS WHO
SNEAK THEIR
CANDY):

NO HALLOWEEN
TRICK OR TREAT
THIS YEAR.

DOUBLE CANDY
NEXT YEAR !!!

November 3, 2020

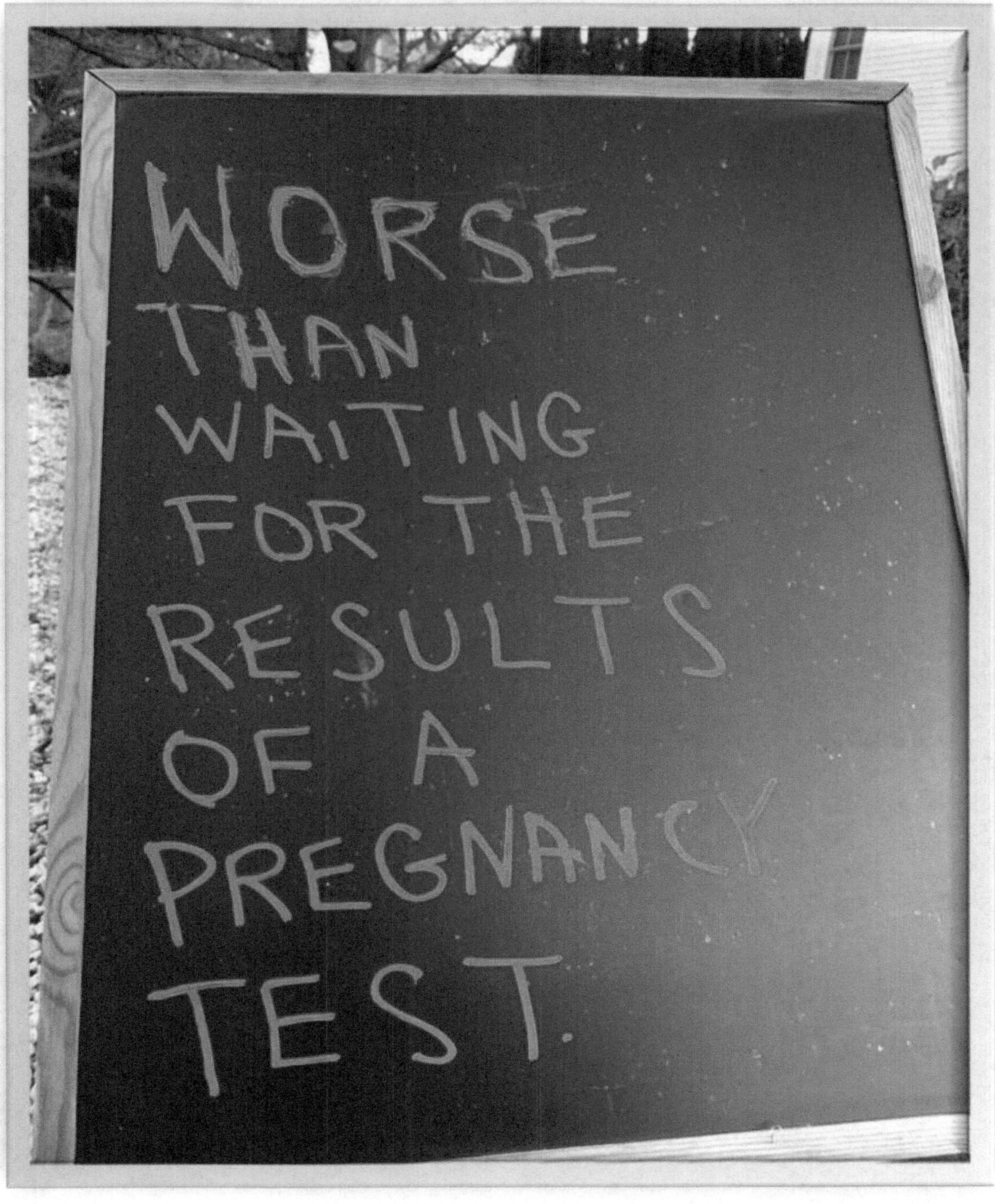
WORSE
THAN
WAITING
FOR THE
RESULTS
OF A
PREGNANCY
TEST.

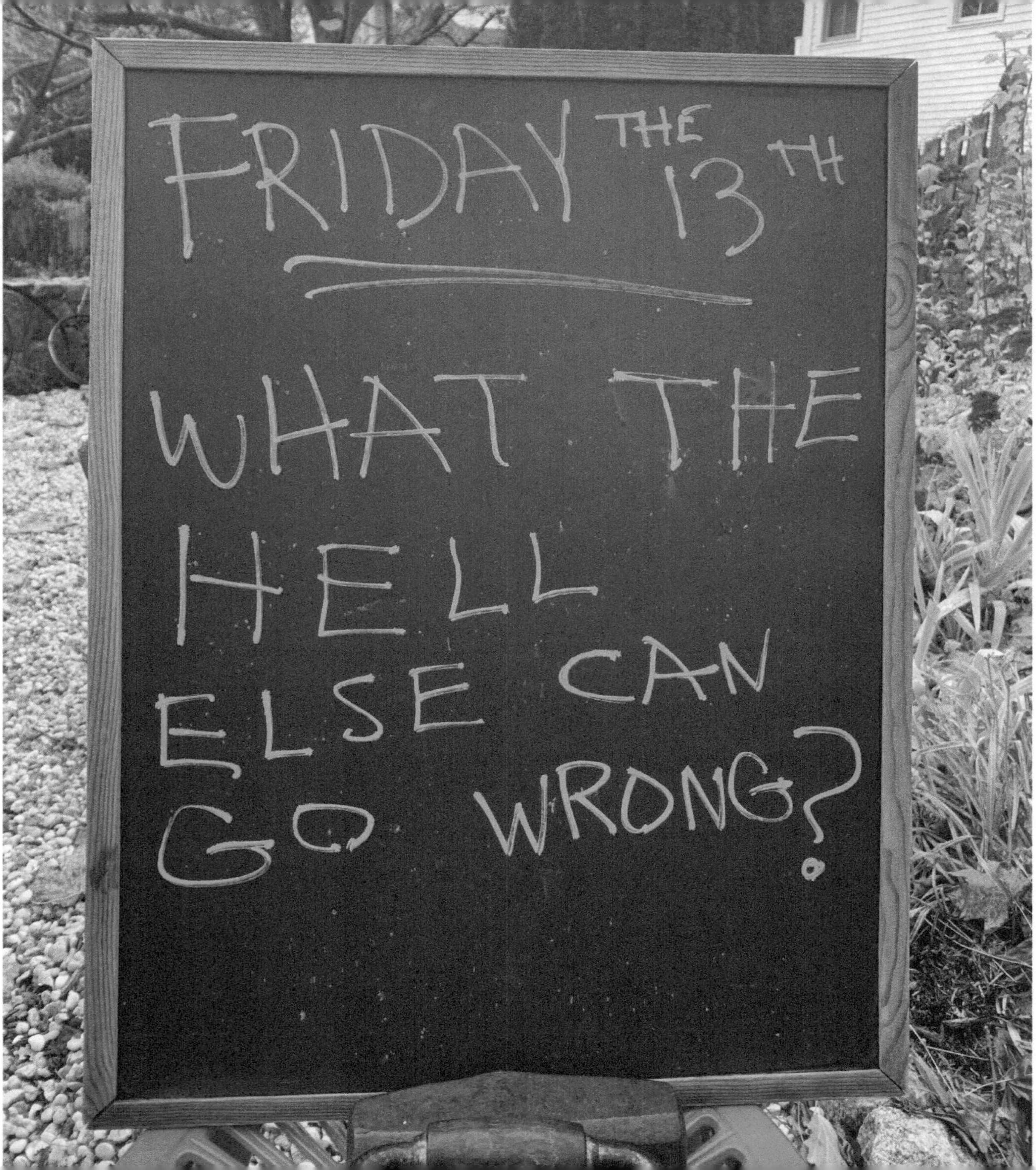
FRIDAY THE 13TH
WHAT THE
HELL
ELSE CAN
GO WRONG?

IT IS THE SONG
THAT NEVER ENDS.
YES IT GOES ON AND
ON MY FRIEND. SOME
PEOPLE   STARTED
^ (MEAN + STUPID)
SINGING IT... (OK,
BUCKLE UP FOR
60 SOMETHING MORE
DAYS OF THIS CRAP.)

HARD TO KNOW IF
IT'S 8 MONTHS IN
SOLITARY LOCKDOWN
OR IF I'M GOING
GAGA...
...A GOOD DAY IS
I ONLY CALL MY
CELL PHONE 3XS
FROM MY LANDLINE
SO I CAN FIND IT AND
I REMBER ONE OF MY
12 PASSWORDS ON THE
3RD TRY....

DECEMBER 2020
-MARCH 2021

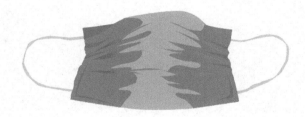

8 months in: no respect left for Republicans. None. Gone forever.

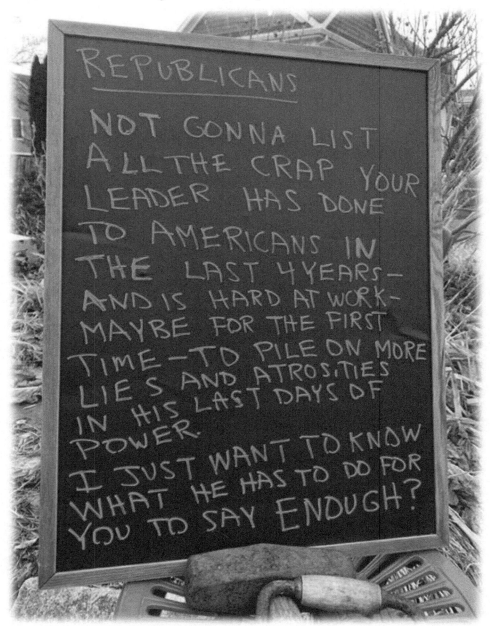

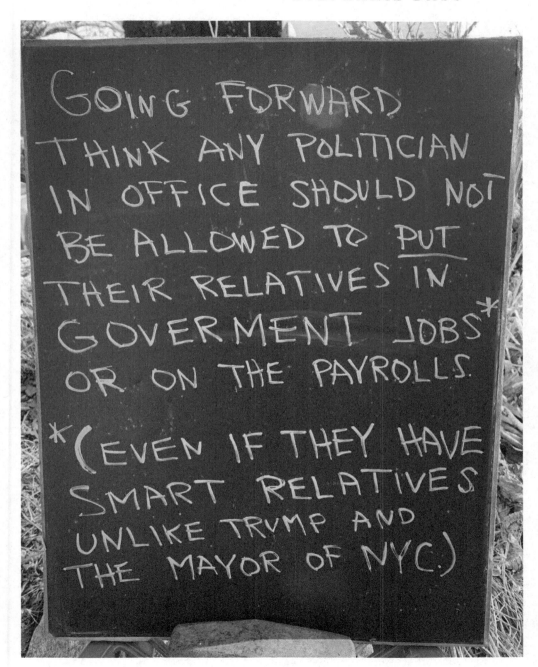

Nepotism in business is bad enough. When incompetent children—and wives—are put in positions of power and either do a terrible job or steal *or do both*, it really pisses me off. I feel it is one of my jobs to speak up where others fail to do so.

Rx: HOW TO WHITE
KNUCKLE LAST DAYS
OF TRUMP REIGN—

LOTS OF
CHRISTMAS
SONGS AND
SAPPY HOLIDAY
MOVIES.

...GOD BLESS US
EVERYONE...EXCEPT
REPUBLICANS.
(THERE'S A LIMIT TO MY
NICENESS.)

TO DO LIST:

1. GET TRUMP + FAMILY OUT OF WH.
2. INDICT TRUMP + FAMILY FOR LOTS OF STUFF.
3. FIRE SPELL CHECK PEOPLE.
4. FIRE PEOPLE WHO SAY MY PASSWORD IS TOO WEAK - AND I SHOULD CHANGE IT EVERY 2 MONTHS.
5. STOP MAKING ANYTHING OUT OF CAULIFLOWER - THE #1 VEGETABLE LEFT ON THE PLATE.

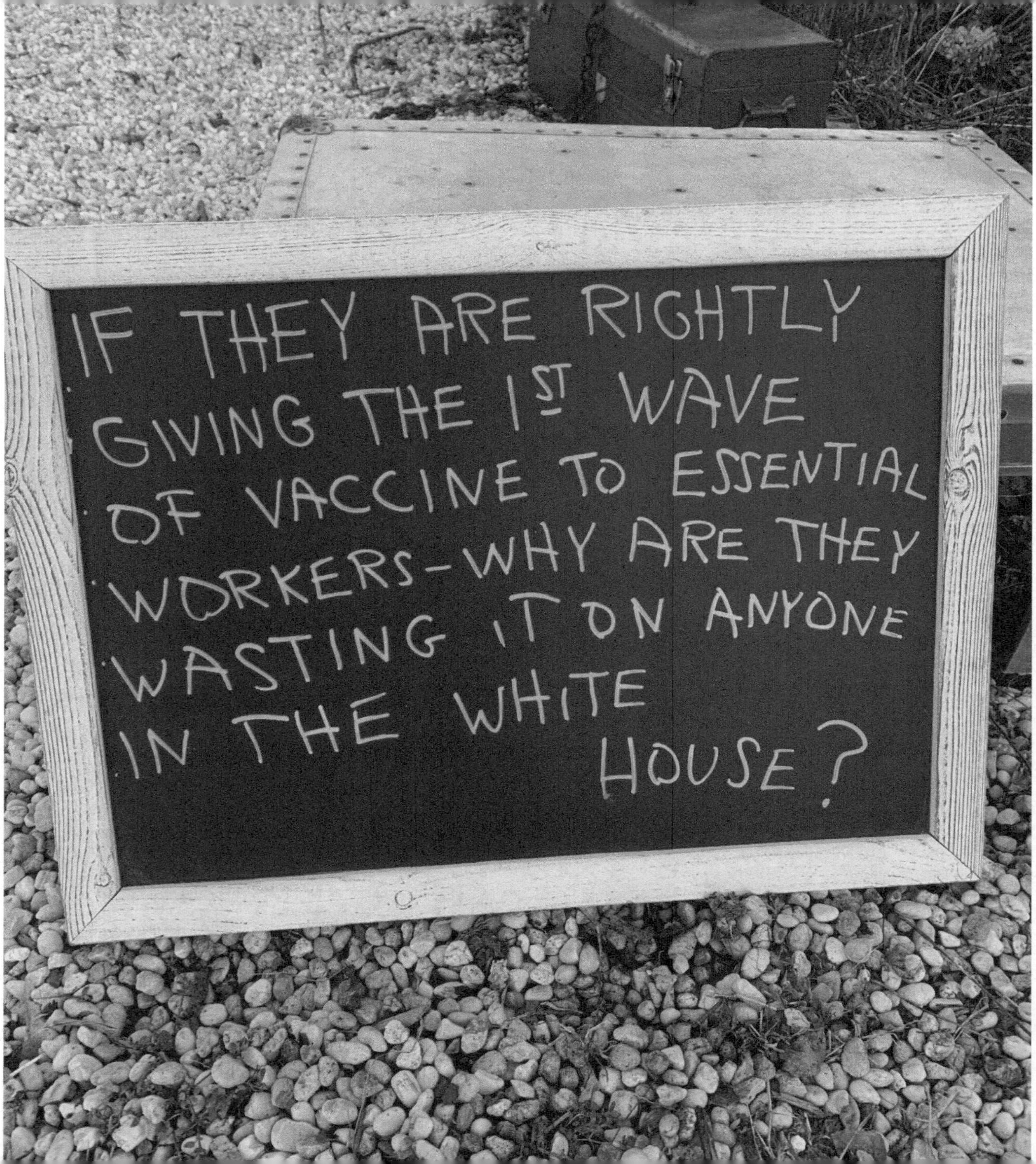
IF THEY ARE RIGHTLY
GIVING THE 1ST WAVE
OF VACCINE TO ESSENTIAL
WORKERS - WHY ARE THEY
WASTING IT ON ANYONE
IN THE WHITE
HOUSE?

PINKY SWEAR 2020 WILL BE OVER SOON

2020
F.U.

We were waiting for the results of the runoff election in Georgia: if Jon Ossoff and Raphael Warnock, both Democrats, didn't win that vote, Republicans would take over the Senate. I felt all hope for any fairness would be lost if Republicans continued in power. They were showing more of their meanness and unchecked greed as the days went on and on. It was a numbers game: we blow Georgia, it was over. The future of the democracy experiment was in peril.

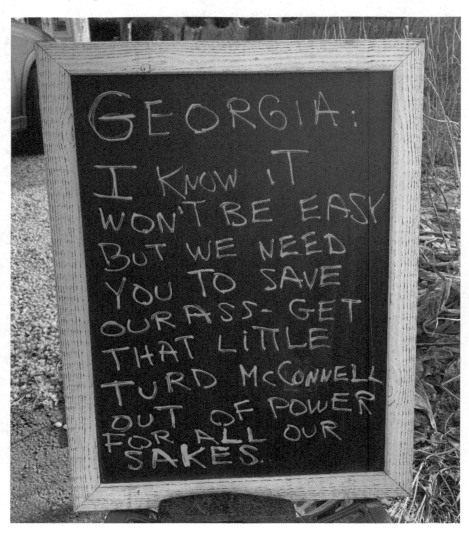

Either we clone Stacey Abrams or we find lots more people to carry the torch. When she lost the mayoral election in Georgia, this woman singlehandedly organized the Black community to go out and vote; she did it by building an organization that knocked on every door and gave rides to the suddenly narrowing polling places in Georgia and she gave America 50 senators and saved our asses. She saved us; I really think she did.

Trump's hate
mob storms the
Capitol

~Daily Mail

Democracy
Under Attack

~TIME

Mob Incited by
Trump Storms
Capitol

~The New York Times

January 6, 2021

Trump Incites
Mob: Rampage
in Capitol Forces
Evacuations; It's
'Part of His
Legacy,' a
Republican Says

~ New York Times

Trump mob
storms Capitol:
President Incites
Crowd to Acts of
Insurrection,
Violence

~The Washington Post

Mob Storms
Capitol:
Lawmakers
reject voiding
two states' votes
after pro-Trump
riot disrupts
Congress

~The Wall Street Journal

"...AS THIS SWEET LITTLE OLD JEWISH LADY COWERS BEHIND LOCKED DOORS HOPING TRUMP DOESN'T SEND HIS STORM TROOPERS TO KILL ME TOO— WE'RE JUST GONNA WAIT 'TIL THE CLOCK RUNS OUT?"

The shirt one of the marauders wore read "6MWE" with a Nazi eagle, which stands for: "6 million wasn't enough." This referenced the number of Jews killed in the Holocaust. It's finally here: we are officially Germany in the late 30s.

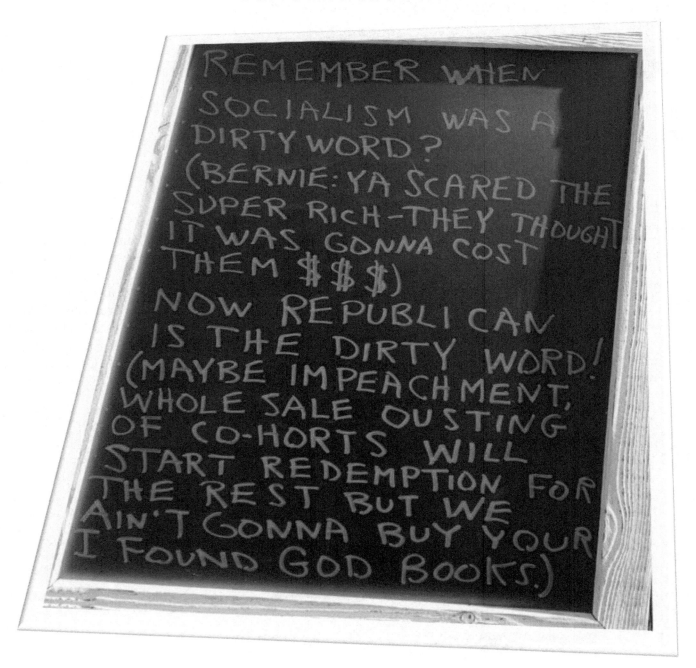

January 18, 2021

Under siege; who are we now?

After the January 6th attack, we were not sure Trump supporters were over trying to take control of the White House. Now the capitol of America was wrapped in barbed wire, and 21,000 National Guard troops were ready for them this time. The FBI announced "insurrectionists," i.e. marauders, were planning another attack during Biden's inauguration. So we waited… didn't happen, but one hell of a surreal time.

January 21, 2021

In the middle of wondering what America is going to look like in the future: the mundane, the trivial and the silly in our lives and our laughter go on.

DETECTIVE,-YOU KNOW WHAT TO DO!"
SECTION 12. DELIGHTFUL ILLUSTRAT
CHARIOTS DRAWN BY TINY SHETLAN
LAST DIVISION OF THE NEW MI
DEST, LARGES
DAY 3
WITHDRAWAL-
NO PACKAGES
FROM AMAZON.
(DO I ALREADY
OWN
EVERYTHING?)

IF I THOUGHT
I'D HAVE TO
BE CLEVER
EVERY DAY
FOR 11 MONTHS
I WOULDA
LOOKED FOR A
REAL JOB.

MONTH #11
ISOLATED
LOCKDOWN:
NO SEX
NO MANI PEDI
NO CLEANING
LADY...
OF COURSE
I'M GRUMPY!!!

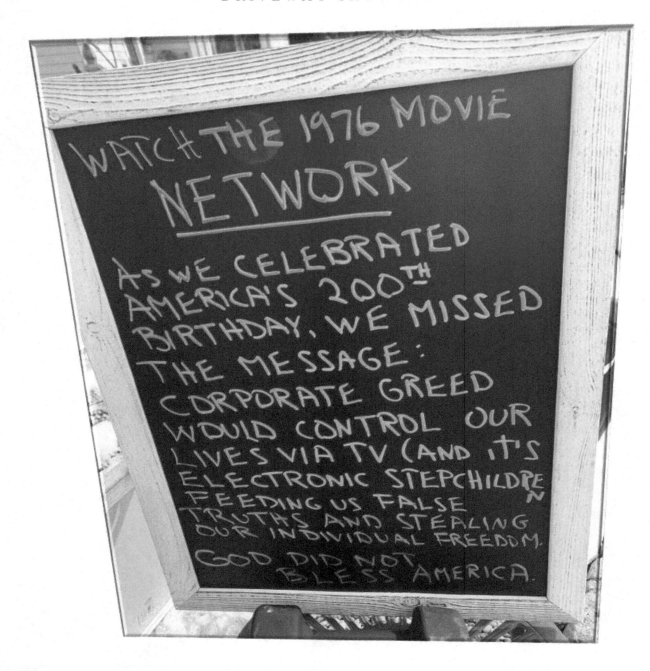

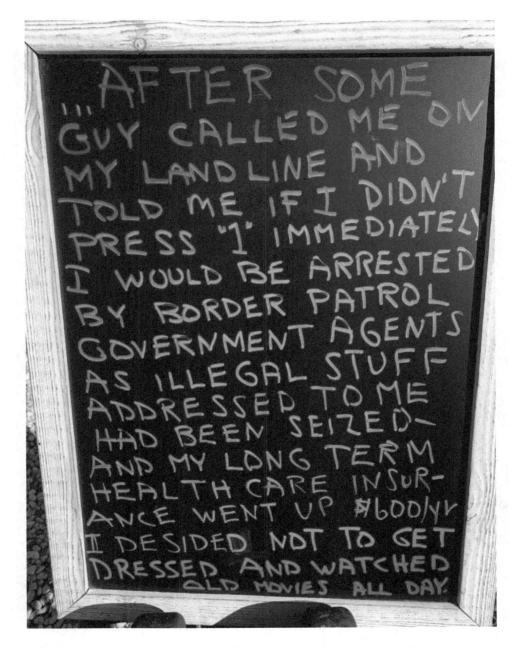

...AFTER SOME GUY CALLED ME ON MY LANDLINE AND TOLD ME IF I DIDN'T PRESS "1" IMMEDIATELY I WOULD BE ARRESTED BY BORDER PATROL GOVERNMENT AGENTS AS ILLEGAL STUFF ADDRESSED TO ME HAD BEEN SEIZED- AND MY LONG TERM HEALTH CARE INSUR-ANCE WENT UP $600/yr I DESIDED NOT TO GET DRESSED AND WATCHED OLD MOVIES ALL DAY.

And in the middle of world chaos, we are still besieged with scams from every electronic device we own.

IPhone just said KEANU REEVES LIKES ME AND FOLLOWING ME ON INSTAGRAM (driveway_showcase). DON'T tell me it's A SCAM - MOST EXITING THING IN LOCKDOWN...

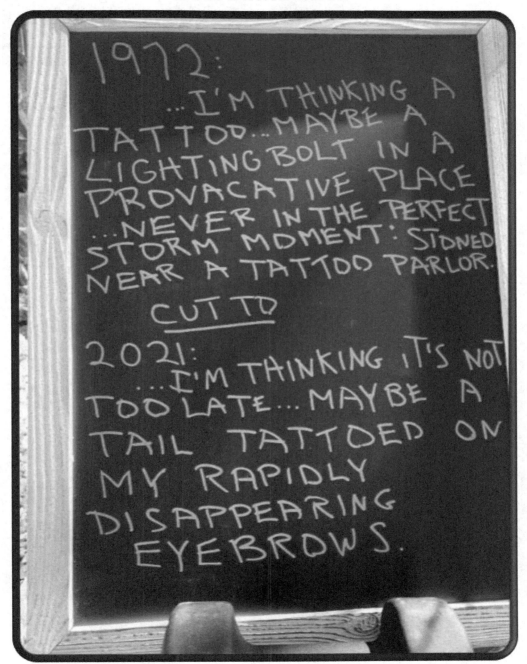

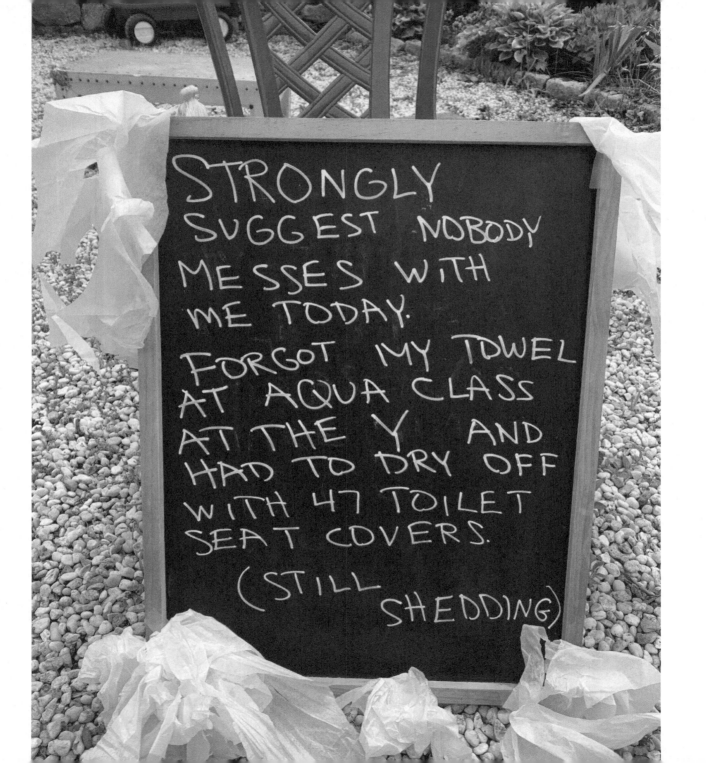

HAPPY BIRTHDAY
TO ME.

ONE YEAR AGO:
• LAST TRIP TO NYC
• LAST I SAW 2 OLDEST
FRIENDS AS WE
ADMIRED HOW GOOD MY
KID TURNED OUT AND
HER KID THREW
BAGELS AT US IN
BARNEY GREENGRASS DELI.
MISS THE GOOD
OLD DAYS.

ACKNOWLEDGEMENTS

TO DANA, MY OLDER SISTER, who got the "smart" label before I showed up—thanks, the default label "funny" was always a much better fit for me.

To Jessie Jane Schwartz, my favorite (okay, only) child: though my original dream of you becoming a rock star bit the dust, your success in business (from your father's gene pool) truly knocks me out. I understand why you won't see me on stage because you've already heard everything I've said 47 times when you were growing up. I extra thank you for vetting my material so millennials get my punchlines and reminding me of gems from our shared past. And while we're not an obvious match—the ADD ex-hippie and the preppie Ivy math genius—raising you has been my greatest joy, not to mention one hell of a gold mine for material. When I called you at 7 a.m. instead of texting and you said, "Never call me this early unless you are actively dying," I was truly proud that some of my genes had snuck in. You are my best work.

To Gary Cohen, Esq. You unwittingly provided me with both my first laugh on stage:

> I'm 70 and lucky: through hard work and perseverance, I don't have to work anymore.
> It took hard work and perseverance to find a great divorce lawyer.

… and a house a ½ block from the beach in Westport, CT. I am eternally grateful.

To Rosie Gates, a wonderful friend. Riffing at my 70th birthday party when I told you my last 5 shrinks said I should do standup, you said, "This is the Universe calling you." Somehow your voice broke through and pushed me onto the greatest adventure of my life. Thank you.

To Suzanne Sheridan, friend, chanteuse and photographer extraordinaire—thanks for bringing style to my book and making me look good.

To Amazon for selling me the $13 book *Mastering Stand-Up: The Complete Guide To Becoming A Successful Comedian* by Stephen Rosenfield. It turned out to be *the bible* of standup, and led me…

… to Stephen Rosenfield, author of the only book I ever read so much I had to scotch-tape it together, and Founding Director of American Comedy Institute in NYC. Your workshops moved me from funny at parties to funny on stage. I feel lucky to have found you and ACI—to be professionally trained by a master was a gift. I still think "joyous communication" every time I walk on to a stage. Thank you for starting me on this glorious trip.

To Ethan Herschenfeld: comic, actor, ~~opera singer (for God's sakes!) and the~~ **best coach at ACI.** ~~You coached me to cut out superfluous words, words that didn't add anything to the setup/punchline format, words that were actually often confusing and distracting to my message.~~ **Thank you** ~~for helping me be consistent in the attitude I wanted to project to the audience, adding nothing that would get in the way of my material; you helped me produce a tight 5-minute set,~~ **for** ~~actually~~ **getting me to a tight 5** ~~minutes, so that in Year Two, when I was really still an ingenue just beginning the journey, you taught me how to both expand a set and acting techniques to memorize a longer set, which is very, very hard for me as I let you know, so when I was on stage in my hometown, Westport, CT? Anyway, I was on stage at The Westport Inn, and I was pretty damn good~~ **.**

To all the comics I met in NYC and CT, in workshops and at open mic nights and at the clubs: what a community I got to join! The camaraderie and support you gave me opened up my life and my mind. A smarter, funnier group would be hard to find. Watching us all get better together was thrilling. The generosity of spirit and advice was both a surprise and a gift. May the world open up very soon so we can all get back on stage and kill.

To Alison McBain, my esteemed editor who I found in my usual way: I asked the first 15 people I ran into if they knew a good one. I interviewed Alison with probing questions:

> ME (1st question): "Do you think I'm funny?
> ALISON: (Laughed...)
> ME (2nd question): "You ever work with anyone with ADD?"
> ALISON: (Don't remember exactly what she said because I can't find my notes; I think
> it's on that yellow piece of paper with the coffee stain that looks like a penguin, but even
> if I found it, half the time I can't read my handwriting.)

You delivered big time—told me I had an arc and a narrative—real, literary terms attached to my year of blackboard S.O.S.s. You supplied the executive skills God forgot to give me and helped me get my story out. You stayed the course, gave me direction, and I wrote a book. Me!!!

And lastly, but really firstly, to my pandemic "audience," everyone who walked and drove by, who laughed at my jokes and left me presents. You caught me writing my truths and stopped to talk to me and thank me for adding laughter to your lives during this how-long-is-this-gonna-last, terrible, terrible year. I'll say it one more time: you kept me sane and made me realize my purpose on the planet: to spread laughter. Thank you.

ABOUT THE AUTHOR

0: born in the Bronx, NY (1948).

4-18: Grew up in Washingtonville, NY. Population 3,000.
Boring. Bolted as soon as possible.

18-19: 1st serious BF. Engaged.
Bolted.

19: Eloped to LA with next BF. Bolted. Lesson learned:
when you make a mistake, get the hell out of Dodge.

20: Arrived NYC. Beginning of lots (and LOTS) of jobs.
Undiagnosed/unmedicated ADD =
short attention span (-)
and exceptional interview skills (+).

18-30: 5 colleges, 4 majors. Graduated: Baruch College, BS
in Journalism, *magna cum laude*.

30: Married engineer. He began to soar up the food chain. I started to morph into Corporate Wife.

32: Moved to dream home: 3rd floor co-op in Greenwich Village brownstone.

38: Had dream baby girl. (Kid turned out great.)

41: Forced to move to Westport, CT. Arrived with curated black wardrobe; did not succumb to clothing with little boats and frogs; did buy $350 microfiber Prada bag. Became Brownie leader.

47: Finally diagnosed with ADD; explained why I always thought everyone else on the planet had an owner's manual but me.

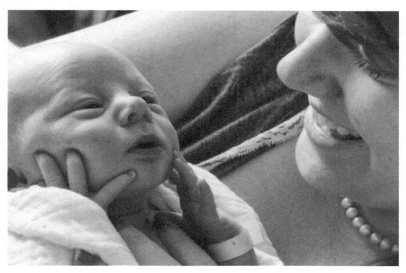

50: Divorced. Reign as Corporate Wife ended; Golden Parachute launched new position as Divorcee in Cottage at the Beach. Bemused.

70: Became Grandma Beach—best job ever!!!

Re-assessed life: decided to launch new career as standup comedian. Debuted at Gotham Comedy Club, Viper Room (basement).

71: Made Round #3 of Funniest Comic in CT.

72: Pandemic plague. World shut down.
In isolation.
Invented DRIVEWAY SHOWCASE.

73: Started to venture out.
Wrote a book.
Still hoping the new world will be kinder.

Made in the USA
Coppell, TX
12 May 2022

77695259R00105